Items should be returned o[r]
shown below. Items not alre[ady requested by other]
borrowers may be renewed in person [in]
telephone. To renew, plea[se]
barcode labe[l]
This can [
Renew
Fine[
in[
be c[

Lea[

An Irish Childhood

By Mary McCann

An Irish Childhood

By Mary McCann

© 2018 Mary McCann

ISBN: 9781912092567

First published in 2018 by Arkbound Ltd (Publishers)

* * *

Arkbound is a social enterprise that aims to promote social inclusion, community development and artistic talent. It sponsors publications by disadvantaged authors and covers issues that engage wider social concerns. Arkbound fully embraces sustainability and environmental protection. It endeavours to use material that is renewable, recyclable or sourced from sustainable forest.

Arkbound
Backfields House
Upper York Street
Bristol BS2 8WF
England

www.arkbound.com

Contents

An Irish Childhood

Prologue

When my daughter asked me to write about my life, I was pleasantly surprised. I thought *who would want to read about me?*

I said as much and she replied "I would!", so I started talking and she started jotting it down. As I never had much schooling I wasn't sure how I was going to tackle the task in hand, punctuation and spelling being pretty alien to me. But as the story was originally for her eyes only, accuracy did not seem to be that important.

This is not a a great literacy piece, but a short story of myself and the tribulations that have carried me through my eighty-six years.

* * *

It was August 2006, just one month before my eighty-sixth birthday. I had just been told I had cancer, given five weeks to live. Well, clearly I did not have a lot of time to complete my memoires. So I thought I'd better get on with it, even if it would be briefer than I had hoped.

Two years earlier, in July 2004, my husband died of prostate cancer, aged seventy-nine. In the last weeks, Katie our Collie dog would lie near him, in the corner of the room wondering what was going on, and why her owner was not sitting in his armchair and patting her as he always did.

She had kept her eyes fixed on him, lying motionless in the bed – neither a movement from his body nor a murmur from his lips. Her eyes would plead for any sign of affection he had previously given, but there was nothing.

The tension of quietness became oppressive. He had lain like this for two weeks - not moving, not making a sound - and she did not understand it. Despite his being so ill he could still hear and would give a little cry when the nurses came to 'turn' him in his bed. He looked so frail after all his suffering and I was glad when he finally died.

Poor Katie seemed to lose all interest in living too, now that he had gone. Like a faithful companion, it was not long before she followed her master. And now it was me lying in bed, with my daughter Jackie sitting on the bedroom nursing chair that I remembered buying in a second hand shop in Muswell Hill fifty-eight years ago.

I looked at Jackie, her head bent over, and I closed my eyes. I was back in County Fermanagh with young limbs and bright hair, lungs that gulped the country air and bare feet that ran through fields and jumped ditches, playing truant from school. The fields were a carpet of flowers in spring and summer with cowslips soft under warm feet.

The winter held its own beauty, no bare feet now though, with the snow sometimes six foot deep. The changing seasons always delighted me, and I remembered light and laughter, sun, rain and snow, and the joy of being young.

Chapter 1

I born on 9th August 1920, a hot day under the birth
sign of Leo, the roaring lion. Little did I know how
much I would need those characteristics as I grew
from a child to a woman. My mother told me that she
was very glad when the birth was over as it had been
a difficult one. I was the third child, a girl after my
brothers Terry and John. My father was a farm hand
at the time and we lived in a cottage on the Henry
McGhee family farm. This is where I was born – a
tiny place called Moneygar about three miles from a
village named Trillick in County Tyrone.

My father, Thomas (big Tom) McCann, was born
in 1889. He was twenty-one when he married my
mother, Catherine (Kate) Donnelly. She was born in
1895 and was nearly sixteen when they tied the knot.
They had my brother Terrence (Terry) in 1916 and
fell pregnant immediately after giving birth. John
came along in 1917 and then me in 1920.

When I was growing up my father looked like a
giant to me: he was six-foot with broad shoulders. He
was very handsome with deep blue Irish eyes.
Although he was a big man, when he danced he was
as light as a feather on his feet, a great hit with the
local ladies! When he and my mother married those
ladies complained that mother had stolen their dancer
out from under their feet.

My mother was very slim, with long red hair that

fell to her waist. She was a beauty with high cheekbones and a small nose. When she smiled her whole face lit up. She did not just smile with her lips; her eyes smiled as well.

As a farm worker, my father had a tied farm cottage and he worked very hard to make sure that he kept a roof over our heads and food on our table. Over the years we lived in several places – Trillick, Tempo, Cavan, Coa, Killee, and finally Killymittan. My abiding memory of that time was the abject poverty, sadness, and illness that accompanied our daily lives.

We had gotten used to moving house in my childhood and the sight of the horse-drawn cart piled high with our belongings became a familiar occurrence in childhood. We did not really have much in the way of goods and chattels so the upheaval was minimal. My father's job dictated where we moved: we went where he could get work.

Although we lived in houses, we were no different to gypsies that travelled around in their brightly coloured wagons. Constantly on the move, I was just three when we moved to our second home.

It was not long before the work dried up and we were on the move once more. This third move was a good one. We began to feel more secure, at least for a while. But it was not to be and we were soon on the move again.

It was a precarious life but the jobs that my father took sometimes came with food or lodgings and sometimes both. As wages were very low, there was always some sort of food on the table. It kept the wolf from the door. But we never felt we were in a permanent home.

Our next move saw father with a live-in position again. Master Murphy, who was one of the teachers at Coa school, owned a farm and employed my father. There were no wages, but there was food and lodgings for us. My father, as usual, never complained, even if the work was hard - his priority was always his family.

One time we had to go to Master McKerney's place, another teacher. He had a poor sick calf and asked my father if he could help out. I went too. I loved being with my father despite my early resentment of my baby brother. Being the only girl made me special in my daddy's eyes, I liked to believe.

* * *

Unfortunately, it has to be said that the idea of 'close-knit communities' was not always true in those days. There was a local man, Joe Love - not a man whom we knew well – who would not help us with accommodation, even though he owned a house and at the time we had not yet become a large family.

So on to our next place: father rented a two-room house with a kitchen for two shillings and sixpence each week. The roof leaked when it rained heavily and I can remember wading through water. We lived up in Killee, an area that was prized for healthy air. We kept an old goat, two chickens, and a crazy goose.

Until my younger brother Eddie was born I was pretty much the centre of attention. After that, young Eddie became a big distraction in the household. I was angry and jealous. I can remember standing over my baby brother's cradle – raging so much that I could easily have rocked him right out of that cradle and killed him. I was suffering from the severe jealousy that many older siblings feel when a new one arrives, although it does make me shudder now to think of the hatred that I felt towards him. But I was lonely, I felt ignored, and it was a big adjustment to make. Now instead of me being the only girl and getting attention, Eddie was! It hurt.

When he grew up my imposter brother got to work at Harland & Wolfe the big shipyard in Belfast. This was more of an accomplishment that you might think since we were Catholics and a job at Harland & Wolf was normally given to Protestants.

At home I remember my brothers cracking nuts on the fireplace. It was here that my mother gave birth to her fourth son, Eddie. Poor families had their babies at home, usually without much medical assistance. Mickey turned out to be a breach birth and the doctor had to be called to assist with the birth. The auld girls, who always had something sitting on the end of their lips, had many helpful old wives tales, such as '*you would not get pregnant again if you breast-fed!'* The evidence all around them should have been a clue that this was obviously not true.

Finally, my father got his lucky break and we settled in Killymittan. His uncle Mickey was selling some land for one hundred and sixty pounds and he let my father buy it from him for sixty pounds. When the contract was signed my father just wrote an X in place of his signature as he could not write. He built us a house with a sitting room and kitchen and two bedrooms in a lovely area, surrounded by rolling hills, with breath taking scenery. This time it was our own and no one could turf us out.

Now Killymittan had once been called Killymittle. This was our last family home, where another seven children had arrived and needed to be fed. Finally, we all grew up and some of us moved away to other parts of the country or England - with the exception of one brother, who, after our parents died, continued to live and work on the homestead.

A new baby sister was next, Alice Elizabeth, although she would be known as Lily. After that came more babies: Etha, Rose, Rita, Seamus, Benny and Charlie, making an extra eight more siblings to the McCann clan. I was told that when I was born I was christened Maureen Anna but I was always known as Mary. I later found out that this was not true; it was just some Irish blarney. It was, however, quite common for people to be called by a different name to the one that they were christened with.

I used to dread mother having another baby. She would pack us off to stay with Aunt Kate at The Mill to collect some milk. When I got back I would make her some tea and toast so that she would have something to eat, and when the nurse came to visit she would have the same. I would make up some water and coconut milk for the baby to drink when it arrived as this was a good substitute for breast feeding, although she continued breast feeding my brother Eddie up until the age of three-years old. I remember him running up to her saying *"I want the wee white cow."* Those breasts did good service over the years: it was amazing that my mother managed to nourish so many young babies.

On one of the nurse's visits pandemonium broke loose after discovering her 'pump and tool bag' (nurse's bag) was missing. It was eventually found with one of my brothers, who had a great idea to hide it. Nurses ruled where babies were concerned and many of them resented doctor's interfering with their work.

Killymittan is only six miles from Enniskillen, the largest town in County Fermanagh and the west of Ireland. It is situated in the centre of the country on an island that separates the upper and lower sections of Lough Erne. The Irish meaning of Enniskillen is Kathleen's island. This was Northern Island's 'Lake District', with dancing crystal clear water and seventy kilometres of fishing. It was complete peace and tranquillity. Sadly, it was later to become synonymous with the 'troubles' that ravaged Ireland, culminating in the death of eleven people in 1987 when an IRA bomb exploded in the town. But it was the other Enniskillen that I knew, the beautiful green and lush land and the home of the well-known Portora School that educated Oscar Wilde and Samuel Beckett.

Chapter 2

Father was an only child born out of wedlock to his mother – Catherine. His father was someone named Thomas Leonard and he was not a Roman Catholic. I heard revelations one day on a walk I was taking with a girl from the workhouse. We started to argue over something silly and all of a sudden she was shouting at me. *"Your daddy's mammy got pregnant by a prossie and they weren't married. He's a bastard!"* The word hung in the air. In the 1930s it was a terrible disgrace to be unmarried and to have a child.

In 1873, at the age of sixteen, my grandmother Catherine had been banished to the USA and her sisters - Rose, Hannah and brother Terrywent – went with her, leaving my father behind with his uncle. After their long journey to the United States they settled, like many other Irish immigrants, in New York. Records show that no less than fifty-seven people with the surname McCann settled there in the 1940s, although my grandmother, Catherine, left Ireland in 1873. The four of them continued to live in New York and one of her sisters never married. The other sister was wed and had two children, Jane and Sam, but they never married either. They lived in Long Island and had government administrative work.

In Ireland the gossip flowed about Jane and Sam saying that they were affluent and had a nice home.

But when my nephew, Seamus, went to Long Island to visit them he found this wasn't the case at all. Their home, so far from being opulent, was actually very normal, mediocre even. Sam was a bit of a drinker and so it was left to his sister to be the main breadwinner of the family. Jane kept in touch with my family in Ireland and visited them once when we were living in Southall in Middlesex.

I am sure that my father must have wondered about his mother and why (apart from one time) she never got in touch with him. He must also have wondered about his father too. When I obtained my father's birth certificate the name of Thomas Leonard was written down as the biological father but then the name was crossed out. I can only imagine how abandoned father must have felt but I never once heard him complain or speculate about his early life.

When Catherine, my grandmother, died it resulted in both my parents being called to Belfast to see a solicitor as my father had apparently been left a 'lock of money' - somewhere around fifty or sixty pounds to her son. Sadly the money never appeared. Word went around the family that his aunt Rose, in New York, passed it on to her son and daughter instead.

I often used to think about my grandmother and how she spent her life in New York. I wondered if she ever thought about her son and how she managed to just forget about him. I have a photograph of her sitting in the back of a big, black car, very smartly dressed and wearing a large brimmed hat and looking quite important. I remember thinking: *where did she acquire such lovely clothes and such a stylish hat?* The car would have been quite special in the 1800s!

* * *

My grandmother's brother was called 'Uncle Mickey of the Mill' because he owned a mill, and stayed on Irish soil. He had developed a reputation for being a bit of a tough auld boy.

He lived in a house that had been the home of a neighbour, called The Danes. Mickey already had one farm nearby and so the rumour was that he was the second wealthiest farmer in the area. He farmed his land in the traditional way, cutting his field of corn with a scythe. Sometimes I would work with him and he would tell me to hold the rod and keep it straight for him. After a week of working with him in the field he would press a sixpence into my hand. My mother disliked him and I cannot say I did either, but the money came in useful!

* * *

At home in Killymittan my father loved to see people ceilidh (gather together) in our house. The men who came played cards; their laughter could be heard and travelled miles around the country lanes. Father was never happier than when he was in company. He loved to tell jokes and spooky ghost stories. His ghostly tales were his speciality and we would huddle around the fire with the turf burning brightly in the hearth, delighted to be terrified by his tales. We had no inside toilet so we would always take someone with us in case a banshee, a howling vixen or a ghost would be waiting for us in the shadows. In fact, Irish people thrive on a good ghost story just as much today as they did back then and are renowned for their love of folklore and superstition.

During our antics as children in the graveyard in Maghercross, legend had it that ghosts liked to congregate there. One such spirit was a Jamestown Lady who was said to roam around the graveyard and Jamestown Road. No one knew which family she came from but reports emerged from some people who walked by.

One such story involved a local person cycling home and passing the graveyard. A vision of a lady in a long white dress appeared to him and then vanished into thin air. Discussion of sightings kept the old folk happy for hours.

In those days people travelled by foot mostly. Otherwise they went by donkey, cart or bicycle. Because of this slow way of getting around, ghost stories and alleged sightings abounded. The banshee was a popular subject of these tales. A banshee is a fairy or magic woman who has appeared to Irish families through the ages. The dictionary's definition of a banshee is a female spirit (vixen), whose wail portends death in a house. To hear a banshee crying out in the night would mean bad news coming to a family. I have to say that in all the time living and being brought up in Ireland and walking home around two and three in the morning, I never saw a ghost or heard a banshee.

* * *

In my mother's family there were six children. The father, Old Eddie Donnelly, married twice. My mother Catherine (Kate) had three sisters - Maggie, Minnie and Alice - and two brothers, Eddie and Terry.

I remember Aunt Maggie well. She was tall and slim. Aunt Minnie was shorter and had very small feet. She wore size-four shoes and she had a child out of wedlock, *wee* Ned, whom my mother unofficially adopted and shared with her mother, helping to bring him up. Later Aunt Minnie married a smallish, darkish skinned man who was nicknamed *the little black condo* - although I have no idea where the name originated from!

In my youth there were many such nicknames, the origins of which nobody would be able to explain. The habit was to name children after yourself or other family members and to distinguish which person you were talking about. People would be called *wee* Ned Donnelly or big Ned Donnelly or big Tom and *wee* Tom. Aunt Minnie and the little black condo carried on to have five children: Sarah, Sheila, Terry, Paddy and Ben. As for Aunt Maggie, she never married anyone and remained a spinster all her life.

My aunt Alice was a very attractive woman with refined small features, resembling my mother except for her height. As a young woman she was working in domestic service for one of the richer households when we heard that she had been taken ill with a lot of pain in her side. She rapidly became worse but because she was in the service of her employers, they would not allow her to go to hospital until she deteriorated and became really ill. By that time it was too late. Her appendix had burst and she died aged seventeen.

Uncle Eddie married and had four children. One of them, John, decided to emisrate to Alberta in Canada to work for the Canadian Mounted Police Force and never returned home to Ireland. He knew my love for dollies and sent me the most beautiful Canadian doll. But as brothers will do, mine smashed up the lovely doll and that was the end of her!

Sometimes my mother would send me around to look after my grandparents, Old Eddie and Ann, so that I could come between them. They lived in a place called Killee, where they had some sort of grocery shop. Old Eddie was a drinker and he would come home after a drinking session and get very aggressive and violent, sometimes even throwing granny Ann and the children out on to the street. Occasionally the police would be called to try and calm him down.

Somehow when I appeared he would calm himself down.

During the school holidays I would stay with my grandparents and they would take wee Ned and me for a donkey cart ride. We would sit on a plank of wood that went across the back of the cart. The two of us delighted to sit up on the seat and trot into town, laughing all the way. One wintry day when the donkey's hooves slipped on the ice we slipped and slid all along the road. Eventually arriving in town, granny Ann would buy *wee* Ned and I a rosy red apple each: the highlight of the trip.

* * *

One of the most popular activities in an Irish community at that time was the ceilidh at friends and neighbours houses. They were a great time with the auld boys telling stories. Granny Ann Donnelly told us a wee story about a group of children getting up to mischief. Her story goes like this:

Some children were ceilidhing at a neighbour's house but they were making quite a lot of noise, so the neighbour told them to go and play outside, shouting 'shut the door on yer way out!' She was in a hurry to get rid of the children so that she could get on with chatting to her friends. Now those naughty children quietly removed the back door off its hinges by unscrewing it, a task that was not difficult in those simpler days. The naughty youngsters carried the door off into the woods and hoisted it up into a tree to lay across the branches for them to sit on. Now one of the little devils decided they wanted to wee and another wanted to defecate (they were very naughty children). These particular children had not been part of the initial shenanigans at the house but went about doing their business. Underneath were two on the door robbers, who, in feeling the first spatters of liquid thought it had started to rain. When shite began to rain down on them, however, they thought the sky was falling.

The moral of this tale was, I suppose, that crime does not pay!

The boys were always getting up to naughty antics. One poor lady had passed away so the neighbours, as a mark of respect, decided to re-decorate her bedroom. This was done with her actually laid out on the bed. So these little monkeys tied ropes to the wrists of the dead lady whilst in bed, keeping the lengths of the rope under the bed clothes on each side of her and then hiding under her bed. When the locals came to pay their respects the boys would tug hard on the ropes and the deceased lady would sit upright in bed. It was a devilish prank to play and the boys were given a stern talking to for *that one.*

Chapter 3

Back then there was no so such thing as contraception. People believed that it was the Roman Catholic religion that fuelled the huge so that the Catholic population would increase. As my mother was a Catholic whether she would have used a form of contraception is debatable. But families grew and grew because the men could not be denied their pleasures in marriage.

My mother was a strong-minded woman and kind to the locals. She had no formal education, of course, but had tremendous common sense. She proved this when one of our neighbours, Cassie Doyle, contracted diphtheria. Afraid of catching the disease, the neighbours would not go inside the house but would leave food and other things on the doorstep for Cassie. My mother, however, was not afraid. She saw a neighbour in need of help and she took action. She disinfected the whole of Cassie's house and looked after Cassie at the same time. My mother had incredible stamina. Sadly as she was put into an ambulance, poor Cassie died. If there was any family in the area suffering with the effects of diphtheria, scarlet fever or tuberculosis my mother would send Nurse Mary - *me* - around to help them out. At just ten years of age it was quite a task for a young girl, and remarkably none of our family ever had any of these diseases that were so common at that time. I believed then and still do now that God and Our Lady the Blessed Virgin Mary were looking down on us.

In fact, by the age of ten my childhood and schooling was effectively over, and I had my duties helping my mother look after the family at home. At the same time I also realised how close I felt to my father; unlike my mother who I had no affection for, nor she for me. I was expected to take on the role of an adult. Later, it became apparent that she favoured my brothers, as she used me like a workhorse. Even when they were grown up and left home she always felt they were helpless. There was no choice in the matter about staying at home and I did not mind - I was not keen on school anyway. In fact I positively loathed going to school. When I was there I hated the relentless bullying from the teachers, and I could never concentrate on lessons. I had no confidence and going to school made me worse.

Nobody worried if a child did not attend school; there was no one who checked whether any of us were attending school or not. The exception was a single school inspector, whom we nicknamed 'the cruelty man', whose job was to visit some of the poorest families in the community. The National Society employed him for the Prevention of Cruelty to Children that became the Irish Society for the Prevention of Cruelty to Children or ISPCC in the 1950's. These inspectors had the responsibility of placing children into Industrial Schools.

Children identified as needing care would be committed to these institutions, often via their relatives. It was common for the parish priest and the Garda (police) to give evidence. We had a solid family unit but some other children were not so lucky. Poverty was rife and children ended up with nowhere to live and no one to look after them. These were children of single mothers who had not been given up for adoption, or whose parents had died or were too ill. Instead of being supported, they were taken up and committed to the Industrial Schools. The state did not address the root causes of poverty but instead children were given up to Religious Orders and the Schools. Looking back now, I can see how lucky we were that we all stayed together.

* * *

Many of the days I was not in school were lost to tasks like shopping, washing babies' nappies, helping bake bread and cooking – boiling potatoes in their skins, cutting green cabbage and collecting the week's eggs from the hen house. The collected eggs needed to be washed until they were nice and clean and ready to take to the local shop that was owned by our neighbours, the McMulkins. Another of my chores was to collect large pails of water from the source near the bogs. I had to feed the chickens and milk the goat, clear the burned heather and tie it up and then put lime in the well and clean it out. No wonder I had no time to go to school!

My mother's strength was not in cleaning but she did make an effort to sweep the stone floor. She would sweep with a besom and a sort of dustpan but there was always so much dirt that it invariably got swept outside rather than being binned. The excess dust would accumulate in the dustpan and the next time it was used would fly all over the house again.

Before we went to Mass on Sunday our mother would wash our hair in cold water using soap as shampoo. That was fine in the summer months but in the winter the icy cold water would actually make your head ache. There was no hot water unless it had been boiled on the range, so anything that was washed got done in cold water. I remember now standing in front of an icy bowl of water, a towel wrapped around my hand like a glove. With the soap in the other hand I would dip my glove into the water and then start to wash. Mother called it *a lick and a promise*. Sometimes though, I was so busy washing the younger ones that I forgot about myself.

Our teeth were cleaned with salt and soot from the chimney and we would crowd around the chimney to get some soot on our fingers. It was a good-natured scramble, and it was family life at that time. I suppose you could have called us the dead-end kids as we bore a resemblance to the kids from a Charles Dickens's novel. And as there was no end to our poverty in sight, it was every child for him or herself.

There was no discipline in the household as such, in the mayhem of our large family. Chickens would run in and out of the house – resulting in stale and fresh chicken droppings being left everywhere. The aroma of the home was certainly nothing like the perfume Chanel No. 5, that I was to love in later life when I got to England, and would become my favourite always. But mother did not seem to mind; I do not think she even noticed.

* * *

My father's fortunes were improving by this time and he obtained a job working for the council on the roads. He got the grand sum of two pounds and ten shillings a fortnight. When he was paid, I would be sent to the shop to get the food for the fortnight. Father would have two ounces of tobacco for his pipe and the Red Rover newspaper. We were still poor but father had his own home, and a good job and we pulled together as a family group. The gypsy life we had lived was now a thing of the past.

Father worked hard for his money. He started seven in the morning and finished at seven in the evening. He would take a couple of pieces of bread for his lunch sometimes, but not always, stuck together with butter. If he was working in Trillick,the doctor or the priest would ask him in to have some lunch. He was a well-liked man, hardworking and on good terms with everyone. In the summer, when the days were long you would see the farmers cutting corn in their fields, often till ten at night. In those days work was what occupied most people's time. For the men an occasional drink with friends or playing cards with neighbours was their only leisure time.

Sometimes my mother would go into Trillick to a jumble sale and Doctor Warnock's wife would give her a big bag of clothes in return for just a few pennies. In springtime for extra money my mother would take two or three chickens tied onto her bicycle handlebars to Enniskillen, a small town sitting on an island surrounded by Lough Erne, some six miles away. She would sell the chickens and get a few shillings for them. The money was saved for whatever the family needed and if some was left over, a bit toward Christmas.

She was grateful for any clothes her children were given, and once we were sent a parcel from New York. Inside the box was a black fur coat and a small selection of dresses. As I was the eldest girl, the coat was cut down to fit me and underneath the hemline showed a white dress. There were also two frocks, two more coats, one plain and braided around the collar and cuffs. None of the dresses fitted my sisters as they were too long and too big and may have originally come from our cousin. We ended up wearing them to feed the pigs in, so I suppose they came in useful after all.

Because times were hard at home, country folk were always there to help one another. My brothers and friends would bundle into someone's old car and go across the border to the Free State, in the south of Ireland. We'd bring back packets of sugar, Gallagher Blue cigarettes, packets of Five, Players, Weights and Woodbines. On our return to the North the border control officials would halt us and ask if we had purchased anything. They knew we had but let us go across, hiding packets of sugar that was for the men to keep up their energy working as labourers, and nylons for the girls which were sold cheaply.

Chapter 4

In 1936 I was sixteen years old. A couple of boys I knew that were slightly older than me supported the Irish Republican Army (IRA) and were members like their parents. These boys were not slow to spot an opportunity and when a lady up the road with the same name as mine died they persuaded me to go and vote in her place as no one in the area was going to recognise me.

Sir Basil Brooke was standing for the Protestant party and lived in a castle near Lisnaskea. He did not agree with giving Roman Catholic people jobs. Then there was Cahir Healy, a Roman Catholic standing for Northern Ireland. My brother Terry remarked one day that he had changed his mind about voting for Cahir Healy or any other politician when he noticed Healy and Brooke leaving a hotel laughing together, seemingly the best of friends. Terry was deeply suspicious that there was not more distance between the two opponents and felt betrayed.

Being brought up Catholic, Terry was born when there was no break-up of Ireland until around 1921, when Northern Ireland was split up into six counties that gave power to England. Around County Fermanagh Protestants and Catholics lived side by side. But the underlying threat to Catholics was that they did not have the right to vote in Stormont, buy houses or be given jobs. Young people aged eighteen upwards started to look at the unfair division. The Protestants were overshadowing the Catholics and they needed a voice. Cahir Healy was there to represent the Catholic working people. But his familiarity coloured his opinion about voting for him.

My father was very supportive of the IRA and was secretly a member of the organisation. Clandestine meetings would be held where people would get together and talk over the latest events. He had every sympathy for what they stood for and what they wanted to achieve. He had many friends, both Catholic and Protestant, and got on well with everyone - but he kept his IRA meetings quiet.

Some of our neighbours were members of the Ulster Special Constabulary, referred to as the 'B Specials.' If they had cause to stop us they would treat us as complete strangers despite the fact that we had known each other over the years. He saw this as Protestant intimidation, as usually there was no apparent reason for us being stopped and searched as youngsters just out for the night at a dance hall. They were intent on exercising their power over the poorest of Catholics who were to be denied their fundamental rights under the British Government.

Quite often the 'B' men would pay a visit to all the Catholic houses in the area, and we were no exception. Early on in my childhood I remember a knock at the door around three in the morning. Mother would panic and out the door the four of us ran. Father would be out at one of his IRA group meetings. These meetings were kept for the ears of the group and they would get together most nights. Father, being on good terms with the local 'B' men, said that *"he wouldn't be late with them."* Meaning he was not slow and quite clever at keeping both sides separate.

After some lengthy discussion with his IRA group, comrades from around the area, along with my father, broke into the local police station and stole a gun. The police stations then were not controlled and secured and so it was an easy exercise. Amazingly they were never caught, given the strict on-going searches and harassment that were a constant occurrence.

* * *

We lived amongst incredible characters and kind neighbours, with good entertaining and craic. As the turf burned on the hearth fire, we all gathered round drinking endless cups of *tae* (tea) and a slice of homemade bread passed under our noses, as we listened attentively to more stories. Father would entertain on the mouth organ. Someone else would join in with the accordion, violin and the bagpipes. Other stories related to other people's problems and jokes about odd people are the one thing you could be sure of. The neighbours spent more time in other people's cottages rather than their own.

The auld boys always enjoyed a drink or two;

there would be arguments and drunkenness, and many instances of falling into ditches drunk, trying to find their way home. One minute fighting hell for leather, and the next the best of friends. There may have been the occasional broken nose and a little bloodshed, but nothing that a good night's sleep would not mend. They would see themselves right at Mass on Sunday. They would make irreverent remarks. For instance, when someone's husband died they might say: *"Put his ashes in an egg timer because he never worked when he was alive so he might as well work now!"*

Or: *"Don't eat curry - the only thing it does for you is burn the arse off you."*

Or: *"No use marrying a woman, you can't take her with you when you die!"*

A couple of our good neighbours were called Paddy and Rose Corrigan. They were always there to tell a ghost story when cailihding at our house. He said that after leaving our house one night, he could see something in white walking along the road. This apparition was a lady dressed in white, who walked with him for about a quarter of a mile down the road and then disappeared.

Paddy and Rose lived in Killee, where we used to reside before moving to Killymittan. He liked a drink and drank more than he should. Rose also liked a drink but only once a month.

Wondering off to the pub for the evening in the horse and cart on, they would climb into the cart in a drunken stupor at the end and the horse would see them home safely. Lucky for the Corrigans, their reliable horse was sober!

* * *

A fascinating story comes to mind which originated from two nuns. They were apparently sitting by the riverbank when a large black car drove onto the bridge and stopped. Someone got out and threw a bundle, wrapped up in brown paper, over the side of the bridge, proceeding then to drive off at speed. The nuns ran over to the riverbank as the package did not quite hit the water itself. Inside they found a child.

The bundle was taken back to the convent, where the nun's reared him and gave him good food and clothing. When the child gradually grew and reached his teenage years, they said that he was very refined, delicate, with the 'cut' of a gentleman - unlike the other children in their care. The story goes that the child was born to one of the Guinness's daughters! This, of course, could be gossip and entirely hearsay. There would need to be actual proof but that never got in the way of a good Irish story!

Another family, The Fossitts, lived in a rather large rambling house. Father knew the whole family and I knew one of the girls. There was supposed to be a ghost who haunted the tree-lined avenue up to their house. They had a relative who used one of the rooms to make coffins. Another room was permanently kept closed and had never been used.

When Mr Fossitts was taken ill one night, he sent his son Harold to call on us. He asked my brother, Terry, to fetch the doctor. When the doctor arrived at our house he asked my father to accompany him as he was frightened to go to the house alone. This fear stemmed from times when the doctor had been asked to visit them on other occasions. The doctor said that when he had arrived one time at the gate to enter the driveway, the horse refused to move and walk any further and for this reason he called on my father.

Father said he never did see the ghost lurking or hovering but on their way out the horse and cart flew down the avenue at such a pace neither father nor the doctor had a chance to look right or left. The horse carried on until they reached the lane and both men released a breath.

It has to be said that in our wee cottage in Killymittan each night, around midnight, without fail, the latch on the front door would lift and make a sound. Mother put this ghostly spirit down to when the house blocking someone's path when it was built: whoever was lifting the latch was trying to continue on their way.

* * *

Looking back at the characters, we had an auld girl come visiting and she was well known for her fleas. The fleabites were visible around her neck and formed the shape of a necklace. She was so dirty that in her cottage cat shite lay under the settee and bed. The smell quite indescribable. She never cleaned her home, dirty auld bitch, so she was.

Another character I would call on was auld Jenny Higgins. She would give me sixpence to buy her a currant loaf and butter from Sarah McMulkin's local shop. When I returned with the bread and butter she would ask me to stay for tea and give me a slice. It was full of fruit and very tasty. Whilst enjoying my tea, just above my head were some wooden beams where the hens would sit. So as I was drinking my tea, the hens would aim and defecate from a height, seeming to take aim directly above my head.

* * *

Sarah McMulkin's shop was the only little shop we could rely on without having to go in to Enniskillen Town. She lived there with her niece, Kathleen. When she needed to make a journey to the bog for some peat to put on the fire, she would harness the dog and attach it to a small cart. Off she would go to the bog! She'd fill up the cart and the dog would expertly pull the little cart of peat home.

She reminded me of the Spanish and Italian country folk as she was always dressed in black. On entering the shop she would often sit by the glowing open range fire, as her little shop was just opposite the sitting room.

Kathleen's father originally came from Killymittan but went to work in Southern Ireland as a police guard. He was a rather stout gentleman and always carried a gun. When his wife passed away he brought Sarah and Kathleen back to live in Killymittan, where they ran the shop.

It was not too long before Kathleen fell pregnant and came to my mother for help. Gossip went that the child was my brother Benny's. My mother sent her to Belfast to stay with my brother Eddie. She was to stay there until the child was born. My sister-in-law helped rear the child, a dear little baby boy. The child was put up for adoption and Kathleen returned home to Killymittan to the shop, never to see her son again. Later on she tried to get in touch with him but he declined to see her.

Chapter 5

My brothers Terry, John and Eddie did go to school but they still helped in the house, often carrying water in white pails, backward and forwards to and from the spring well. All our water came from the well. It was crystal clear, clean water with no chemicals. As we had no toilet, we used the fields to do our business. There we would wipe our backsides with grass or newspaper - whatever was at hand.

Meal times were haphazard, with the usual scramble for a chair or a place on the floor to eat. Always starving hungry mealtimes and the tension was a welcomed sight! Mind you, tension often exploded. Sundays were different. Perhaps because it was a holy day and after Mass we were allowed to sit down at the table and eat and behave ourselves.

Because we were so friendly and welcoming, there was a constant stream of visitors calling at home. What little we had, we shared.

I remember an incident when my sister Rosie (Rose), who was not at that time living at home, made a big black pot of rice for the family. My mother's cousins called in to see mother and found Rosie there, alone. Without hesitation they fell on the rice and ate it all. My sister was distraught and shouted *"the divil choke yers!"* The rice had been prepared for us but had all been instantly swallowed. Because there were so many of us, mother had trouble hearing her visitors when they came. She would bellow *"Have a piece of manners, God Almighty knows I'll kill yers, get out of the road."* With that she would shoo us out the door and that was a great result as we could play and not do any of the chores. We loved having visitors.

One of them, Doctor Warnock, always enjoyed coming to our house to have smoke and sharing craic with father. My brothers would hover and fight around him as he smoked his Gallagher Blue cigarettes, hoping to get a dog end. Their faces were the picture of horror when he threw nearly half the cigarette into the fire.

* * *

In between mother's pregnancies and my chores I occasionally managed to turn up at school. The Coa School two miles walk along the road, although I would often take a short cut over the hills. Whatever time I set out, I always managed to be late, getting up to some mischief along the way. I was what you would call a *wee rascal* – anything to get out of attending school! Then when school was done I would dawdle home knowing that when I got there, chores would be waiting to be done. I would stop and watch the cows and their calves in the fields; it felt good to be free on those times I was alone with no one asking me to work or study!

* * *

Although poor as church mice, our diet was pretty healthy. On a Friday evening our father could bring us home a dozen herring for meal time. As good Catholics father always insisted that we eat fish on a Friday.

We always grew our own potatoes on our land. We did not make our own butter, we bought it from a neighbour, a pound in weight, delicious and creamy and home-made. We also purchased tea, sugar and large Spanish onions. The farmer would give us round cabbages, as big as footballs.

In stormy weather, when lightning flashed and thunder rippled through the air, salmon would swim from Lough Erne up river. My father would try to catch as many as he could. This activity would be done late at night, and after a long day at work; somehow, he would muster the strength to stay up and catch the fish. He knew if he was caught he could be prosecuted and fined for poaching. Inevitably someone did report him, but such was his standing and popularity in the community that he was let off with a warning.

We burned peat on our fire and when it was time to stock up we would take a donkey and creels to the bog and take what we needed. Back home we would stack it neatly in the barn. The smell that the peat gave off as it burned permeated the house and is etched on my memory. It is a smell I can still recall today.

For supper mother would put the potatoes, or spuds as we called them, still in their skins, into a big black pot and boil them. Keeping the skins on kept the spuds fluffy and flavourful.

Every Wednesday my mother would bake homemade bread in flavours like white, treacle, fruit, ginger and wheaten. An eight stone bag of flour would last us several weeks. Golden meal, sometimes called Indian meal, was sometimes mixed in with white flour. We had food that was good for us and this golden meal also fed our chickens!

Oatmeal was used to make Stirabout, a combination of oatmeal and water mixed together. That was our porridge but without milk.

When we had it, I loved Irish potato bread - made with cold mashed floury potatoes mixed with a little flour and salt fried with bacon. That was a luxury when we had it. Another big favourite of mine was sweet holes (doughnuts).

We drank our tea out of jam jars or brown pots without handles. I still remember my mother giving me a shilling to go to the shop and buy four of those brown pots.

The only transport we had was a donkey and cart or bicycle. Father used the bicycle to get to and from work. He was passionate about greyhounds; he loved having them around. I cannot count the number of times he turned up with a greyhound that he had bought from someone. After chaining the animal up outside the house, my mother would then untie the dog and let the dog wander when my father wasn't looking. I think she thought it cruel to have a dog restricted in that way.

When the snow fell deeply in the winter and my father could tack rabbits easily, he would kill them and bring them home to be skinned. He showed me how to do this and hang them up outside the door. Mother would cook them with carrots, parsnips and onion gravy. He also hunted hares as well. Hunting them saved us money, which could be spent in other ways. To this day the snow brings back memories of those hard times of poverty and deprivation. Rabbit has never appealed to me since then.

In the countryside feral cats were everywhere. While they were useful for keeping down vermin, just like us, there was not a lot to sustain them and many starved. There was no such thing as neutering so kittens were another constant problem. Young though I was, I totally accepted the idea that it would be kindest to drown them at birth, to save them from a very hard life and eventual starvation. I would drown litters, one by one in the lake. I did this without turning a hair. That was simply country life – and death.

We children were lean and feisty, like L.S. Lowry's match-stick men. I can remember one argument over a chair I was having with my brother in front of the fire. We were tugging it back and forth when he suddenly let go and I fell backward onto the fire. I screamed and another brother, Terry, quickly pulled me out. My father had been passing the door with a hay bale and I remember him throwing it down and rushing to my side. My mother had just come back from shopping and scooped me up, placing me in-between two pillows and turning me from side to side. The doctor was called and when he looked under my skirt I was badly blistered. I was very lucky that my burns were not worse. I still have the scars now.

When your childhood is set in poverty and troubled times, decent clothes are a rarity. The only time we saw nice clothes were on the children whose parents could afford more, going to Sunday Mass. My sisters and I had to wear hand-me-downs and make-shift garments. I remember promising myself that one day I too would wear nice, clean clothes. But even without smart threads we still attended Mass at Coa Chapel every Sunday. We were never allowed to miss it.

Flour bags formed the basis of our wardrobes. When mother had finished using the flour bags she would lay them out flat on the table and pour washing soda over them. Then she would roll the bags up, soaking them in water for a couple of days and nights. The sacks would be boiled in a big black pot, then rinsed. Once the sacks had dried out she would make vests and petticoats for us girls. The tops were buttoned front and back, and that was us *sorted!*

* * *

Christmas was a time of year that we all looked forward to. A different feeling would overshadow the day-to-day drudgery. Mass and the birth of Christ would be a focus for us all. As far as food went, things were only a little different - although we often had more fruit to eat at Christmas. There were no presents but we would get an apple and an orange in a sock, if we were lucky.

We had no Christmas tree, and in fact I had never seen or heard of one at that time. The local shop often gave our family a current loaf and some fruitcake. Our neighbours were good to us as well.

For Christmas dinner my mother would kill a goose (after she had fattened it up for the occasion), cutting off its wings to use as dusters around the house. We wasted nothing! She would make stuffing using white stale bread, cinnamon, mixed spice and chopped onions mixed in a bowl with some salt and butter to bind the mixture together. Vegetables grown by us - swedes, carrots, parsnips, turnips and corn - would accompany this meal.

We grew many varieties of potatoes – Champions, Irish Queens, Kerr's Pinks and others that were all delicious to eat. King Edwards, Blue potatoes and Epicures that grew very large were given to the *auld* sow (pig when we had one) as food stuffs for other animals. I have seen White's potatoes sold in England but to us in Ireland they were only fit for animal food. We had our standards then.

Chapter 6

As children we were like any other youngsters, always acting the goat. A little way from Killymittan a group of wee cottees and wee cubs (girls and boys) would congregate at Maghercross Cemetery, where the well-off folk would inter their dead in the 'vaults of heaven'. These vaults had stone lids that could be pushed aside with force. We children would combine our strength and try to push the lids off the vaults so that we could peep inside.

Some of the vaults contained glass caskets with flowers on them. To our shame, we would have competitions to throw stones inside and see who could break the glass casket. We did not realise how utterly disrespectful we were being to the poor souls who lay in the vaults. Poorer, local people were also buried there, although not in such grand graves. The churchyard was also said to be haunted.

History had it that the Coa area was part of the Parish of Derryvullen with a chapel and graveyard at Maghercross where the local people were buried. The original chapel burned down in 1537 - at the same time as the church in neighbouring Kilskeery. During the Jacobite Wars King William's army was billeted at Trillick on its way back to Enniskillen in August 1689. While they were camped a blacksmith in the army died and was buried at Maghercross graveyard.

Unaware of the history, we children would recite

the rhyme:

"The pope, he was a gentleman;
He wore a watch and chaining;
And King Billy was a beggar;
And died in Water Lane"
(King Billy being at the battle of the Boyne)

* * *

As we grew up dances at Coa Hall became our main source of entertainment. The dance hall was close to the chapel. We would go along to the dance at about ten or eleven at night and not get home until two or three in the morning. The priest would always sit at the door of the chapel keeping a watchful eye on the young people. But we had no alcohol and we would dance and dance, reel after reel, until we were exhausted.

We would throw a leg over our bicycles, or take someone else's when they were not looking, and ride home in the pitch dark, with no light to guide us. We always had an ear cocked for the banshee who was supposed to be lurking in the darkness.

* * *

Mother seemed to have a cure for any ailment that you could think of. I remember her boil remedy very well. For a boil on the body, usually the back, she would melt carbolic soap and mix it with sugar. She put the mix in some linen and applied it to the boil, bandaging it in place up around the shoulder. The poison would ooze out like toothpaste out of a tube. I think this was a very healthy way of dealing with it, allowing the poison to be expelled from the body rather than absorbed into it.

Adding some castor oil to some brown paper and then applying it to the chest area was her treatment for coughs. This created a heat that would be medicinal. As for the patient wrapped in brown paper – they looked like a badly wrapped parcel ready for posting!

Applying Iodine to a tooth helped with toothache. But mother had another remedy too. She would fill father's smoking pipe with tobacco and then warm it on the turf fire. When the pipe was hot she would put it in the child's mouth and say *"smoke, smoke, smoke!"* This would make us quite dizzy and the pain would gradually subside – well, that was the idea. I think that the real idea was to keep us quiet and stop us whining for a while!

For indigestion we were given baking soda in water and sprains were treated with chicken weed, a weed that grew in-between the potato drills. The weed would be roasted in a frying pan, then put on a cloth and applied to the area that was sprained and then it would be bandaged.

To keep us warm at night in a house that was always cold and had only one peat fire, mother would take the huge black lids that had been on the cooking pots, wrap them in rags, and put them into our beds for us to warm our feet on. That would go well until the rags came off and we would shriek as our toes were burned on the hot lids. There were other hazards of sleeping by 'top and tailing' in one bed, because if anyone wet the bed you would wake up in a swimming pool!

Mother suffered terribly with migraine and her self-treatment for that would be to tie a scarf very tight around her head to achieve maximum pressure. That seemed to ease the pain. However, mother wore a black beret over her hair summer and winter. I think this was a shame as it hid her lovely long red hair but it was a way of keeping her head warm.

I think I should say more about my dreaded school days. Far from being the best days of my life they were definitely the worst. The school I attended, Coa School, had been established in 1820. It was built in stone and lime and was thatched. It was 18 foot long, 12 foot wide and 7 foot high. Both Protestant and Catholic children attended.

There was another school in Killymittan that had been established in 1830 and had 36 Catholic and five Protestant pupils. This school was, however, little more than a mud hut and eventually collapsed. The children that attended there ended up going to the Grove and Coa schools and it turned out that most Catholic children went to Coa school and Protestants to the Grove school.

Coa school was two miles away from home. We had several teachers: Mistress Murphy and Master Woods, Master Woods, and so on. The school was tiny and so that the classrooms could be divided there were some sliding doors.

Master Woods one of the strictest teachers and he beat me black and blue with his bendy cane. He frequently left marks on my body from his vicious beatings on my shoulders and on my head, which frequently brought up welts and bumps. My crime was having difficulty with my sums.

I was not confident at school and the constant bullying by the teachers made things a lot worse. I was, at heart, a free spirit and I resented being confined and bullied. Phil Doyle sat in front of me and when Master Woods would give us our sums I would give mine to Phil. I warned him that he better do them right or I would *kill him*. He always did, but I did not learn anything.

Another of the punishments that Master Woods delighted in inflicting on me was to stand in front of him at lunchtime and demand I recite the Catechism of Christian Doctrine. This tested my memory, which was never the best. I remember stumbling through a recitation of a prayer called The Angelus. Master Woods would start off by saying: "The Angel of the Lord declared unto Mary."

I would reply "And she conceived of the Holy Spirit, Hail Mary full of Grace, The Lord is with you."

This would go on until I was all but exhausted with the effort of remembering it. He thought that his way was the best to guide me through the learning process.

I did try to learn my Catechism by heart; the corners of my book were worn and stained with thumbprints from the times I had read it through, over and over again. I would be nervous and make mistakes and then he would hit me.

Between his treatment of me and the time that I was kept off school to help at home, my school career was very much less than glittering. But there was one prayer that I always registered in my mind: The Lord's Prayer. *That* I would always say out confidently at morning Mass.

It seemed to me that Master Woods did not appear so cruel towards the other pupils who received better treatment. He had a son called PG from his first marriage and even he took some beatings. PG eventually studied to be a priest.

It was a horrible time, despite having friends like Bridget McGovern, who was very bright, because I also had tormentors like Greta McQuade who for no reason at all would hit me.

My sister Lily was not a great fan of school either and found learning hard. She suffered at the hands of Master Woods as well, who would tell her *"You'll never be good at anything and you'll never go far."*

Many years later, after her move to London, my

sister ran into him again when she was visiting Ireland. She told me that she saw him for what he was then: a small village country teacher. She thought *"I've been much further and seen more of life than you have ever seen."*

Master Woods lived five minutes away from the school and his wife would prepare sandwiches and a container of tea for his lunch. He also would have two slices of toast and dripping which his wife would bring to the school for break time. Seeing him with this tasty treat, my only thought was to *shove it down his throat.*

Mistress Murphy could also 'bash you bandy', but then in the next breath would ask me if I would kindly carry her books home for her and then ask me in for a cup of tea! She even gave my sister Lily and I some clothes and these would be dresses that we wore in the summer time. I suppose that she felt sorry for the dead end kids.

There were other random acts of kindness. A classmate would bring in twelve cream yellow yoke Easter eggs to share out. Not everyone received one though.

I remember one time when the teacher was giving a party and invited only her friends along. Some of us were passing her house and they overheard the music. She had made a jelly and blancmange and put them in moulds, which were left on the windowsill to cool down. Well, it was inevitable. We snatched the sweet treats from the windowsill and we were gone. This was our revenge for not being invited.

Those same boys and girls spent much time trying to capture Master Woods in rhyme, and this was the best they came up with:

> *"Coa School is a nice wee school*
> *Built with bricks and mortar*
> *And the fault I have to it*
> *Is the humpy old Master.*
>
> *Master Woods, he shits his duds*
> *And puts them out to dry*
> *The crows began to pick at them*
> *And the poor Master cried."*

The boys in particular were full of such devilry and made up many a unflattering rhyme about our teachers and our school.

My brothers even worked at the school cleaning the toilets for three shillings between them. The toilets were actually buckets full of urine and faeces and my brothers had the unenviable task to dispose of the contents. They would shovel the shite over the wall, where it would be absorbed into the ground. They had no intention of digging a hole to bury the excrement.

Chapter 7

We had Mass every morning, but in the afternoon at around three thirty every day we had to memorise certain prayers. My friend Bridget would stand in front of me and if I needed her help I would pull at her skirt. If she did not help me I would threaten her with a punch. Obviously I learned something from Master Woods, even if it was only how to bully other pupils.

Luckily my rough treatment of her did not affect Bridget and our friendship later on in life. We ended up going to England together to visit North London.

I can remember sitting in the school yard at break time and us all chanting:

I was sitting when I received your letter
The more I read, I shit the better
The ground being bare and short of grass
With your letter I wiped me arse!

We would laugh and laugh. Granted it was not the finest poetry ever to come out of Ireland but it was a release from the hard discipline that we had to put up with!

There was no school uniform and in the summer we did not even wear shoes to school. We were lucky to have skirts to cover our arses! During winter Master Woods would hand out clogs donated for the poor children by those whose parents could afford to buy them shoes. These clogs were comfortable. I was also given a navy jumper and a navy skirt.

I can remember very well running along the roads in bare feet. But the traffic of heavy carts often took its toll and broke up the rocky surface, leaving sharp edges to cut our fee. It we did get a cut, we would run down to the river to wash the blood off our feet.

Once my mother gave me her shawl, pinning it around my shoulders to keep me warm. The way to school included going over the stepping-stones of the river. A storm had raised the water level and on that day these stepping-stones were underwater. As I tried to walk across I lost my footing and ended up in the water. My brother Terry pulled me out. Everything was soaked, including mother's shawl.

I knew I would get a good telling off when I got home. This resorted in a wallop around the head with the wet shawl, added to the other wallop which I received for smoking behind the chicken shed, which my brother Eddie tattled to my mother.

On the way home from school we often used to cut some of the fern bushes, fashioning them into bicycle shapes so that it looked as though we were riding bikes home. Although times were hard we were happy-go-lucky and had a lot of fun in those childhood days. I can still recall feeling of the damp in my hair and nostrils as I walked to school through the country lanes, and the smell of peat burning on the fires of the cottages I passed, mingled with a strong smell of cow manure wafting through the cold air.

* * *

As a family and martialled by mother we all had to attend Mass at Coa Chapel every Sunday. Hopefully neat, clean and tidy. A few locals would pass us by in their horse-drawn carriage or carts, who enjoyed turning their noses up at us.

Father Lappin would take the service. We also went to confession once a week to confess sins, although as a child my 'sins' were more like mischievous deeds.

One day Father Lappin was hearing confession and actually came out of the confession box because he heard me chatting to someone instead of sitting quietly reading my prayers while I waited my turn.

"Mary McCann, will yer quit yer talkin now!" he cried.

This was not the first or last time I had been in trouble with Father.

* * *

Before we left for school each morning we would grab a slice of bread and wrap some paper around it. Often, before we had reached the front door, the bread would have slipped out of the paper and the chickens would make short work of it. We were always late and usually ran all the way to school. We carried a lidless jar of cocoa water and, even though we ran, tried hard not to spill any of it. On arrival at school we could put the cocoa on the heater to keep warm. All the jars were lined up on the heater and resembled a fair ground game – hit a jar and get a prize. Lunch time was cocoa time.

Sometimes I would accompany Helen McCusker, our neighbour, and we would walk to school together. She was a fat lady with swollen legs and she had no help at home apart from their son. Walking with her would slow me down, though it did not really matter as I was always late with or without her.

There were some light sides to school. I was very good at sports and could run faster that most of the other children. I enjoyed camogie and hurling especially. Playing sports was different from the pressure I felt when I tried and mostly failed to learn from books. This was my escapism.

I was not above a bit of petty theft in my youth either. Once I needed a pencil and book for school and I sneaked my hand into father's trouser pocket when he was asleep to steal a sixpence.

Normally, it was customary for children to finish their schooling at the age of fourteen - but by the age of ten, eleven or twelve I was out of school more times than I was in it. Eventually one of the Masters realised my poor attendance. He advised my mother not to force me to go to school nor punish me for staying away. "Just let her be," he advised.

I had been relegated where education was concerned. It was a difficult time, bullied by the teachers, then being hit at home.

However, living in the countryside was an education for us children - with all the wild animals and wild birds that we lived amongst. When the swallows came we would try to shoo them away but our mother would tell us to leave them alone. *"They are like gypsies, they'll leave us by nightfall,"* she would say.

Beauty and wonder were all around us, and there were fields of the most vibrant yellow cowslips. In the hen house bantams with wee chicks would snuggle into my neck.

I can still hear the sound of the corn crack when the corn was being cut in the field.

Us children, like the animals around us, mostly survived on our wits. One favourite occupation was watching the frogs spawning in a lake nearby. I loved the feeling of the frog spawn running through my fingers like semolina.

We were cruel to those frogs by lighting straws and putting them up their backsides until they exploded. We had no idea that this was cruel; we just saw it as having fun. The boys would also make use of pig bladders when one of the animals had been slaughtered, blowing up the bladder and using it as a football.

* * *

Around 1936 and aged sixteen it was time for me to leave my little Killymittan home and make my first move to Kiltimagh – to a convent. This was near the famous 'Shrine of Knock', a religious area amongst the Roman Catholic population. This was where Our Blessed Lady Mary, St Joseph and St John the Evangelist appeared at the Church of Knock in the 1800s. Many Catholics would make the pilgrimage to Knock every year to say a prayer when they felt the need for help in their everyday lives.

So before setting off on my new venture my mother needed to sort out some clothes for me and wanted me to have a new coat that she could ill afford to buy. I was quite a plump girl, with tree-trunk legs and thick ankles. Whether it was all the potatoes I ate or plain puppy fat, I cannot be sure.

As luck would have it, a neighbour had a tatty, well-worn coat without inside lining. So my mother gave it a good brush and turned the coat, which was a good quality, inside out. Now the reversed side was showing, and off I went to the convent with a nearly new coat.

I arrived at the convent scared, lonely and frightened. Who could tell how I would adjust to a change that meant living with other people in another institution, having to suffer discipline which I had always fought against. A different way of living; I was certainly in for a new experience!

Chapter 8

I cannot recall how many female borders were housed in the convent, but it seemed many. The nuns had full responsibility for the running of the school and mother superior was the *boss*. For my sleeping quarters I had a cubicle that was off the main dormitory that I shared with one of the nuns. She slept on one side of the cubicle with me on the other.

The staff were awakened at five thirty in the morning. We carried out some duties and attended Mass at seven o'clock, still rubbing the sleep from our eyes, followed by breakfast at eight o'clock. We had lunch at one o'clock and we took our evening meal at six o'clock. Bedtime was no later than nine-thirty. At lunchtime we took our meals in the kitchen with the live-in staff and not, of course, with the borders.

One lunch-time I was trying to force my teeth to chew some meat. The blood was oozing out of the raw meat, making my stomach heave and turning me off eating meat forever. The nun supervising us noticed my lack of appetite and that I was not eating this awful red stuff. She proceeded to raise her black-sleeved arm up in the air and came down with a wooden stick – *slap* - straight across my hand. Not once but twice. I got the message first time round – unlike my stomach! It took ages for that meat to digest.

So from then on I worked out a plan to avoid eating more meat. When the nun-in-charge was not looking, I passed the meat onto another girl's plate when her head was turned. Luxury serviettes were not given to us like the nuns', otherwise I could have hidden it. To this day I have never liked or eaten meat and the smell whilst cooking.

If I had mentioned the incident to my mother, in a letter home, she would have dismissed it as moaning.

In my opinion some nuns were capable of unnecessary cruelty – and forcing us to eat food we could not stomach was one of them.

The nuns took their meals in the main dining room. Their table was laid with a well starched, crisp white table cloth and serviettes. They expected a high standard.

The convent was self-sufficient and the nuns had a large orchard of fruit trees. They grew their own tomatoes, together with a selection of vegetables like potatoes and turnips. They raised chickens, pigs, cows and calves. They consistently produced all their own food with the help of laboured men to help. They wanted for nothing. At least we were also fed fresh vegetables, which I enjoyed.

Most nuns were very strict. I felt I wanted to send some religious little prayer cards home as I was in Knock. One of the nun's intercepted the envelope and removed my letter and prayer cards. Today, I would have said that was just a selfish gesture and not related to God at all. They were more concerned that in my letter I might criticise them.

Poor families were often forced to send their daughters to work in the convent so that they could be trained to become a priest's housekeepers and live-in maid. When mother mentioned to a neighbour that I had gone to the convent to train, she laughed and commented: *"Yer Mary will never make a priest's housekeeper, that's for sure."* I was known to be such a wee terror! Looking back, people were always good at putting me down.

Our duties at the convent were enough to put you off housework forever. Sheer slavery. The first job of the day was to take a walk down the long dark corridor with its cold flagstone floors to the school kitchen, where the boiler needed lighting to heat the building.

I was already freezing as it was winter. At five thirty in the morning I was just about awake enough to carry out the task. I'd wander down to the kitchen as if I was sleep walking, and still exhausted from the day before. The constant tiredness and lack of enthusiasm never left me.

The convent had pipes, but of course no radiators as they were not used then.

We then cleaned the boarder's dormitories, including the toilets. Then it was on to washing and ironing clothes. We had to wait on the boarders to make their life comfortable. Whenever we had visitors at the front door we had to stop what we were doing and go and answer it - then one of us would inform the nun. It was not the nun's place to greet people at the main door.

One morning, fatigue taking its toll, I was so exhausted from working in a cold environment that I actually fell asleep against the pipes in the dining room. All of a sudden I looked up with bleary eyes and saw a vision of a black shape coming towards me and could hear the footsteps in the distance. No, it was not a ghost or a Penguin.

The nun caught me snoozing and told me to get back to work. At least she did not rebuke me. Though some were strict and harsh, two very kind nuns come to mind: Sister Joseph and Sister Michael. They were renowned for their kind, gentle approach and we always looked forward to seeing them.

Night times could be very eerie. Along the dark, cold corridors we would go and suddenly there would be the footsteps of a nun, looking for you, her prayer beads rattling.

Girls like me were expected to make life easier for everyone, but not for the staff. Respect was something that was not relevant to our poverty stricken life.

The staff and I were allowed outside once a week on a Sunday, with the nuns. This would be the afternoon walk. Two nuns walked in front of us, then the boarders, then us, then too nuns chaperoning behind. We looked forward to this routine and it made a change from staying in every day. It was not that different from being a prisoner really.

One of the girls working alongside me was always hanging around as she made it quite clear that she liked me very much. I did not recognise the signs until she asked if she could sleep with me and then I realised she was a lesbian. I was young and scared that another girl would approach me in this way. This was also about the time I found myself in the toilet wondering where the blood in my knickers had come from.

I was a late starter with my menstruation and my mother had not explained this important change to me. I was not quite sure what was happening. This necessitated a visit to Sister Joseph. When I explained she kindly put her arm around my shoulder and reassured me. From then on until I reached the age of sixty-eight, when I had to have a hysterectomy, I always had cramps and heavy periods.

I cried almost every night into my pillow, quietly, so that the sister could not hear and in the morning my pillow would be damp with tears. I was just homesick; I wanted to return to Killymittan.

The unhappiness I felt at the convent turned me toward Our Blessed Lady for spiritual comfort and as I was living close to Knock, I would recite the Hail Mary Prayer sometimes, alone in the dormitory. It was the second prayer I could remember apart from the Our Father without floundering:

Hail Mary, full of grace, the Lord is with thee;
Blessed art thou among women,
And blessed is the fruit of thy womb, Jesus.
Holy Mary, Mother of God, pray for us sinners, now,
And at the hour of our death, Amen.

* * *

The duration of my work experience at the convent (if you could call it that) was six months. I had been so unhappy there that the Mother Superior made contact with my mother and said that Mary "*needs to return home*".

If only my father had let me go to America instead of working in the convent, it would have presented an opportunity. Instead my mother needed me at home to keep house and look after the younger children, but was quite happy for me to leave and go to the convent. I decided that if I married I would only have one child. I packed by little bag and left.

Whilst attempting to write about my experiences in the convent, I happened to mention them to a homosexual friend of mine who was unaware of my background then. He proceeded to tell me that he had been sexually abused by one of the Christian Brother's at his school and went on to explain about the book called "Suffer the Little Children", and posted me a copy. An interesting, but very sad, book.

It talks about Ireland's Industrial Schools,

Reform Schools, Convents and Orphanages. It covers the physical and sexual abuse suffered at the hands of Catholic Religious Orders who ran the institutions post 1992. The book was written by authors Mary Raferty and Eoin O'Sullivan, whom I am sure will not object to mentioning their names.

I felt my time spent in the convent at Kiltimagh was hard enough to take but after reading this, the horrors that those poor children endured, I realised that in many ways I was quite fortunate.

Chapter 9

It was around 1937 and I had just turned seventeen.
After a short spell at home I was packed off again
from Killymittan, but this time it was not a religious
prison I was going to but a slight variation on a
theme. A live-in position, with some freedom. I
wondered what was in store for me.

I was starting my first real job as a scullery maid
for a Lord and Lady Cullum at their mansion house.
This experience was to take me through to a year or
so in to 1938-39 when the Second World War was
about to break out.

They were situated on a very large estate just on
the outskirts of Enniskillen, near my home town.
There was a gate house just at the entrance and a long
drive leading up to the big house, which were
common to large properties of that time. At the end of
the drive stood two coach houses, but unusually no
horses were used on the estate. There were four staff
working there including the scullery maid – me.

My chores were scrubbing and cleaning the
kitchen range until the sweat ran down my face. It
was hard work, I can tell you, and thoroughly boring.
I would give out a whistle and sing – anything to take
my mind off the job. After the kitchen range came the
task of cleaning the kitchen work surfaces, sink, and
the highlight of the day was getting down on my
hands and knees to scrub the stone flagged floor. It

was the largest kitchen floor I'd ever seen.

The parlour maid's duties came next, who laid the tray for breakfast and took it up to the Master and Mistresses' bedrooms. As they slept in separate rooms this meant laying two trays and two lots of breakfast. One for his Lordship and one of her Ladyship. The parlour maid's duties consisted of laying the dining-room table for lunch and dinner, duties I took on when she had her day off. The cook carried out her own duties and cooked for all of us, including the gardener.

On one occasion Lord Cullum had a friend who had died and the burial was to take place on a Sunday. It was the cook's day off so I was ordered to bake some scones, which I had never made in my life before. I was very nervous. Luckily the cook had given me instructions prior to her day off so I just about managed it.

It is common practice in Ireland that, when a funeral takes place during the day, a wake is held at night and often continues until dawn. But on this Sunday, in the billiard room, many people attended and scoffed all the scones. The maid's bell rang constantly for more tea. They drank, what seemed, gallons and they must have left the gathering bloated. *Serves them right,* I thought. Not a scone or crumb was left on the huge plates. We were looking forward to the leftovers, but never got a bite. I cannot have made too bad a job of those scones!

The house was very beautiful and the rooms ostentatious. Each was painted and decorated with glorious gold, with fine furnishings.

The Cullums were childless. The pink room belonged to Lady Cullum and the red one was Lord Cullum's, whilst the green and blue bedrooms were the guest's bedrooms. Every room had a chaise longue and an antique wash stand with a large china wash bowl and jug. All the rooms had a wooden four-poster bed. Lady Cullum would refer to the colours of the bedrooms when she wanted them cleaned, and I mean *cleaned*. She was very fussy and always inspected your work after you had finished. Not one speck of dust should remain, nor any piece of furniture be out of place. The paintings and mirror frames were cleaned with a very fine brush.

The staff lived in the basement or below stairs and I shared a room with tiny windows on the same level as the garden, with the parlour maid. Luckily neither of us was claustrophobic. The servant's quarters consisted of two rooms. One for us, and one for the cook. The gardener lived with his two sons in the gatehouse. We awoke around six in the morning for a delightful wash in cold water and soap, then dressed in our brown uniforms, white aprons and caps, ready for the day.

The work was truly arduous: we swept the concrete front steps, polished the hall, cleaned the carpets, lit the boiler (which had coals underneath that needed to be carried in and stoked up). We washed the boiler lid that was practically the weight of a man. When the washing was finished and to be carried over to the butler's sink, we then put each item through an antiquated big ringer and placed it on the line to dry. I did the ironing on Tuesdays.

On Wednesdays after lunch we cleaned the silver, large trays, candlesticks, cutlery, and muffin dishes in the dining-room. This room was adorned, again, by antique furniture: red velvet curtains and Indian carpets on highly polished floors. If you were not careful you could slip. On one occasion, I lay on the carpet and the parlour maid grabbed hold of the front two ends and pulled me around the dining-room table. We had to get our fun somehow and this relieved the monotony of everyday life.

Breakfast consisted of porridge, bacon, eggs for the staff and on Sundays the dinners were wholesome. I did not partake in eating meat though because of my experience in the convent. Still, we were given exceptionally good food.

The Cullum's meals were served on time and could never be late. At eight o'clock breakfast was served in the dining room. Coffee was at eleven o'clock in the morning room. Lunch was served at one o'clock in the dining room, as was dinner. Afternoon tea was taken at four o'clock in the morning room. On special occasions they used the drawing room. On Sunday, if they had visitors for afternoon tea, it was normally served in the billiard room.

We had every other Sunday off or a half a day on Thursday. If any of the servants wanted to go out for the evening there was a curfew of nine-thirty. I remember one incident when the parlour maid and I had been out for a few hours for a bit of light relief. Lord Cullum complained that we'd left the lights on, so he decided to unscrew the outer case of the light switch and disconnect the electricity. That meant that when we had a free night we had to stumble around in the dark to find our way back to the bedroom. We were never allowed to use the main red-carpeted staircase, only the servant's wooden staircase. We knew that Lord Cullum would be lurking around until we returned home. I wasn't keen on Lord Cullum as a person but he did have the decency to pay his staff well.

Lord Cullum loved to spend his time in the garden wearing his rubber boots and was always eager to help the gardener. He was never afraid to get his hands dirty. Lady Cullum, on the other hand, would sometimes take me in the car to drive down to the end of the avenue, where we would both climb out. She would cut the flowers, which we would then put into a large straw basket, return to the car and drive back to the house.

At one o'clock I would ring the hand bell for Lord Cullum to come and have his lunch and leave dinner for the three black and white gun dogs on the steps outside.

Lady Cullum was a large, tall woman, attractive, very gently spoken and very well-mannered whenever she asked any of us to carry out a task. Her maiden name had been White before she married, a very ordinary name and without status until she married Lord Cullum. I could not say this of his Lordship. He had a tendency to be short-tempered, sullen at times and not very approachable. We liked communicating with the Lady of the house and not *Billy Goat Gruff,* as he was nicknamed. He could be disagreeable and arrogant.

On our day or half day off Margaret and I would share a bicycle - a blessing, as otherwise we would have had a long, long walk up the avenue towards the house. I would sit on the handlebars. The walking we could do without as we did not need this sort of exercise. On occasion, and not often, we would like to go to a dance to let our hair down. We would ask Lady Cullum, but we still had to be back for nine-thirty so only spent an hour or so dancing.

We also had tremendous laughs with the gardener's son. He was always joking and one night dressed up in a black jacket and hat, calling to the house around the servant's quarters. It would be dark and late and we would have to get out of bed to see who it was. *Rata, tat, tat.* We would answer in our night gowns, shivering with the cold, but there would be no one in sight. He loved playing ghostly tricks - a real *auld eejit.*

Lady Cullum was such a kind and a thoughtful

person, a real lady. I remember her going to visit a girl who was living in the workhouse. Her name was Teresa. This poor girl was young, lame and pregnant. It was terribly sad. The father of her baby had left to find work in England. Lady Cullum wanted to employ someone to take my place when I eventually moved on to pastures new. I had been with them for over a year now and I wanted to go to Belfast to work and from there, hopefully, to find work in England and make a life for myself. As my mother did not want me at home I could see no advantage in staying in Ireland. So Teresa came to work for the Cullum's.

It was quite common then for employers to take on young girls with a child; she then had an obligation to the family because of taking her in and employing her at the same time. Her options would be the workhouse or a live-in domestic servant. At least she would feel safe with her child.

I kept in touch with Margaret, the parlour maid, after I went to England by writing. Apparently she told me Teresa continued working for he Cullum's for some time and when Lord Cullum eventually passed away, he left her a little legacy. This proves that he had a kind heat after all, even though he was a tight so-and-so at times with the lighting. But it is also fair to say that he was the best employer that I had come across in Ireland, when it came to feeding us and wages. He paid and fed us better than anyone else.

Until I had worked for the Cullum's I had never set eyes on a telephone. This is how ignorant I was at nearly nineteen years old and coming from the country. But then we did not have any toilets at home, let alone a telephone. Having a telephone, God almighty knows, that was some luxury.

Soon, though, it was time to pack my case and move on.

Chapter 10

It was not long before mother had me off her hands once more. The rest of the children were not taking over with helping at home. I was off to the big city of Belfast. This was my second position after leaving the convent and the Cullum's. My brother John was getting married to a lady named Cissie who had been employed by a Canon Oldham as a housekeeper.

I am sure mother hoped that all the time spent in the convent would be put to good use now and calm me down from the terror I used to be. This meant I would be employed as a live-in housekeeper at the Old Rectory for the Rector, Canon Oldham and his wife. They lived in a lovely Victorian house, with flagstone floors. His study overlooked the front garden and road, in Stormont on the outskirts of Belfast City. He was not a very pleasant man - rather brusque, direct and quite off hand to his staff. He was as tough as a whalebone and an *auld* sod. His wife could only be described as a right auld bitch, so she was.

As we were in the throes of the Second World War and food was rationed and times were hard, my brother John had his marriage marriage service at the Old Rectory and the Canon married them. It did not cost any money and they had to be grateful.

During my time at the Oldham's my brother and Cissie were trying to find somewhere to live in the County Fermanagh countryside. An opportunity finally presented itself from a neighbour, Harry West (not to be confused with the Northern Ireland MP). He had land of seven or eight acres and offered John the chance to have two railway carriages for twenty-pounds. They paid the money, moved in and started a family.

The space was tight with a kitchen, small range to burn turf, and one bedroom. In this tiny space they somehow managed to bring up six children. One day a man came calling at the railway carriages selling a gas cooker with a Calor Gas cylinder attached and they bought it. Eventually they managed to have a house built, which gave them independence, and in time along came another three children. At least they had a life together and Cissie was not beholden to the Canon and his wife.

So life was to start with the Canon. He employed me as a full time staff member. No other staff were employed and I had my own room in the basement. There was no heating in the bedroom. I wore a black outfit with an apron and cap and was always cold. Mrs Oldham would dress herself in the *press* (airing cupboard). The only other heat in the house was the fire in the sitting room.

I cleaned and cooked and tried to remember what I had learnt in the convent. The lessons were cemented in my brain.

Breakfast was served at eight o'clock in the dining-room. The Canon would be sitting at the table dressed in the same old beige cardigan that he wore every single day. I never saw him wear anything else as a substitute. He was a wizened auld man as his wife was a wizened auld biddy. I would make them tea, toast and porridge followed by lunch at one o'clock every day. She taught me how to make homemade soup which they had for lunch.

Because food was rationed, so were the eggs and other produce (but some farmers were generous to accommodate the Canon). The menu in the morning or at dinner time never varied. The evening meal would be bacon, vegetables, potatoes, onions and some eggs.

As for me, breakfast, lunch and dinner was combined with *porridge, porridge, and more porridge,* nothing else, which I ate alone in the kitchen. I suppose the man of the cloth felt that this was enough to give me to eat while they ate the best food. I needed to keep my strength up but this clearly never occurred to his wife. God almighty knows us poor morsels needed more food! Or at least a change in diet. The aroma of cooking bacon, fried onions and vegetables wafted under my nose. At times I was starving hungry, but I knew that the Oldhams would not give me the drippings from their noses.

There was only one bathroom with one bath. I was not allowed use it. There was a separate toilet and wash hand basin where I washed in cold water. This was not a problem for me because in Killymittan I was used to washing from a white metal bowl and jug of cold water. *Who heard of a bath*? So if we smelt or did not wash ourselves properly it was just too bad. Maybe that is why today I have never liked taking a bath, have never liked swimming or the water. The water always scared me, but in time I was eventually able to sail the Irish Sea once I moved to England.

The lawn at the back of the house was the size of a tennis court, which I had to cut. For this I was paid a half-a crown. Another task was to bury the Canon's pet fish when they died. Mrs Oldham ordered me to bury the fish directly under Canon Oldham's study window, so they were close to him. He had a fish tank that was his pride and joy. These were sad occasions for the two self-centred humans.

No, they decided *not* to serve the fish up to me for a meal! Well, it would not have gone down well with *porridge*.

It was early in the morning and I was putting on my uniform when I noticed red spots on my fingers and midriff. At first I did not know what they were, then realised I had caught scabies - a contagious skin disease caused by a parasite. Off to the hospital I was sent, although it was really the workhouse. There I was given a bath – yes, a bath that nearly scolded me, as it was far too hot. One of the staff in the workhouse applied cream to the affected area. Sometimes the itching was so bad that I would get up in the middle of the night to apply the cream, which lay on the table beside my bed, leaving me short of sleep and tired the following morning. I was allowed to have four days off not cooking, but wore gloves to do the housework.

I was soon back to the routine. It was a mystery where the scabies originated from as I never went out at all, never had a break, and worked seven days a week.

By this time I realised I was due for a change of job. *Once again, it was time to pack my back and leave.*

* * *

Belfast in the 1940s brought us girls plenty of boys and young men who were in the forces, mainly sailors coming off the ships. The sailors would bring girls all types of presents: nylons, chocolate, Senior Service cigarettes. When my sister Lily worked in Belfast for a short time, she chatted to a sailor and asked him if he smoked.

"No", came the reply.
"Do you drink?"
"No."
"Do you eat grass?"
Silence.
It was all light-hearted fun.

Later on in the year 2004 I recall a telephone conversation with my sister-in-law, Cissie, who lived in Trillick.

We talked about old times and reminisced about the people that we used to know around us in Ireland and having a bit of a craic. We then got onto the subject of a pop group named the Bee Gees and how we both enjoyed their music. It transpired that when I was living in Ireland, just up the road from us, was a place called Kilskeery. I remember having a boyfriend whose surname was Murphy - a good old Irish surname. His Christian name escapes me.

It transpired that he was the father of Robin Gibb's wife, of the Bee Gees. The world could not be smaller and be both chuckled. Robin and his wife still went home to Kilskeery to visit her homestead. Cissie said that at one time Mrs Gibb wanted to buy her father another house but the old man wanted to stay in his old home, where I believe he still lives today, according to my nephew.

Chapter 11

The opportunity now arose for me to find work and live in the big City: London. I felt I was on the road to freedom, but that complete freedom had not arrived just yet.

Every position I took after departing from the convent was living-in and this continued until I was twenty-seven, when I would marry.

Bridget and I had registered in Belfast at an employment agency who specialised in domestic positions and nannies for families in England. The agency gave us an address of a lady whose sister was married to a Professor living in Highgate, North London, called Doctor Boyd. And she would help us find work. She informed the agency that when we arrived in London, if we were not happy with our respective positions, we could contact Doctor Boyd. Well, we had nowhere to go so when we arrived we went straight round to see Doctor Boyd, who without hesitation found us live in jobs.

I first travelled to England by ship, to Heysham, and then took the train to Euston Station with Bridget. Surprisingly this was not too frightening to us as we had previously worked in Belfast so were used to a city. We were both off to pastures new and I was put in touch with a Jewish lady, Mrs Newton. It was a live-in position and nanny to her two children. She had been a dancer before she married but gave this up. Her husband was a Harley Street specialist and they lived in a very large detached house in Golders Green, where many of the Jewish community resided. As I only worked for this family for three months I never quite knew what her husband specialised in. But later it was alleged that he had been sent to prison for performing illegal abortions.

I was given a bedroom next door to the two young girls, Carol and Valerie. When I was not the nanny I was the cleaner. Many domestic duties were thrown at me and I was given no time off. It was living in seven days a week once more. There was no such thing as job satisfaction, job security, or unions to protect your interests. Nor was there any sick or holiday pay. We had to be grateful, earning little money and being exploited. It was the same auld story.

The Newton's daughters attended Aida Foster Stage School, in Temple Fortune, Golders Green. It was here that I had the greatest experience of my life watching Jean Simmons dance. She was fourteen years old then. Not long after seeing her there she starred in the film *The Way to the Stars*. And I also saw her at the pictures in *Give us the Moon,* where she acted as Margaret Lockwood's precocious sister. She was incredibly pretty, with long black hair. What a vision! In time, her success would make her become a great actress, in particular for her role in the musical

Guys and Dolls opposite Marlon Brando, a film I never tire of watching.

When my sister Lily came over to England she eventually went to live near Crouch End. A small world to know this is where Jean Simmons was born!

* * *

The tension in the Newton household between the so-called lady of the house and me was nearly at boiling point.

One chilly, cold morning I had overslept and Mrs Newton took it upon herself to push open the bedroom door and throw the alarm clock at me in the bed. She missed me, thanks be to God. Had she not, I could have ended up staying in bed with a massive headache or acquired a huge lump which would not have gone down well with her ladyship.

I put this down to her artistic temperament. She would then retreat to her bedroom; one had to grin and bear it.

She was a horrible woman, spoilt and prone to tantrums and a real madam. Well, let's say a *bitch*. What else would one call her?

Usually I was left a written list of jobs that needed doing. On their mother's instructions at breakfast time I was to give the two girls porridge, but they would go and throw it down the toilet and tell their mother that they had eaten it all up! Valerie was a very sweet-tempered child and I preferred her to Carol, whom I could tell even at a young age was following in her mother's ill-tempered footsteps.

Then one afternoon scandal hit the Newton household. Mrs Newton was having a clandestine love affair. Her boyfriend bought her a mink coat as a present – for sexual favours, one might say. On this particular afternoon, when she had returned home with him, I overheard them arguing in the lounge. I was in the kitchen and I saw the boyfriend dragging this beautiful, shiny mink coat along the floor like a large furry animal trailing behind him. He made towards the front door and the fur coat vanished.

I was envious of her colourful, stylish expensive shoes that were hand-made. What I would have given for a pair of hand-made shoes like hers or even just one item of her stylish clothing! As children in Ireland, we had no choice but to wear clogs. Something I learned about working for the middle class people was their appreciation for good quality clothing. This would give me expensive tastes in later life, which I also passed on to my daughter.

Mrs Newton was so appreciative of all my hard work that when Christmas was upon us she generously gave me *six oranges as a present*. I did not know whether to laugh or cry but eventually I laughed. They had everything and you had to be content with nothing.

At least she gave me the opportunity of seeing Jean Simmons dance on the stage. I followed her film career, which was a great privilege and a memory I do not wish to forget. Yet my patience was exhausted working for this awful woman.

* * *

It was time to get in touch with Doctor Boyd once again. I explained that I had been unhappy working for Mrs Newton and had left with nowhere to live and needed another live-in position.

As a matter of urgency she immediately put me in touch with another of her friends, Mrs Hudson, also residing in Highgate. She had just given birth to a baby boy. After the birth she had become quite poorly and needed a nanny's support with some extra help at home. I was lucky enough to get Bridget a job working with me as well. This was going to be about four months work.

Mrs Hudson was involved with broadcasting on the radio. I found her a pleasant and polite lady. I looked after her son, Benjamin, and Bridget did the cleaning.

It was then suggested that I take baby Benjamin away to Salisbury for a couple of months so that Mrs Hudson could rest at home with Bridget taking care of her. So baby and I left for Salisbury for a two-month holiday to stay in a large house and garden belonging to Mrs Hudson's grandparents. I was left purely alone to look after dear Benjamin. The grandparents also stayed in the house but did not interfere with my duties in any way. We only had a visit from Doctor Montgomery, who came from London to check on the baby and ensure all was well.

Finally the two months were up and I returned with Benjamin to Highgate. We were not wanted anymore and it was time to move on again.

Realising our dilemma, Mrs Hudson managed to find me employment with a friend – namely, Mrs Erika Rapon. So on to somewhere new.

Mrs Hudson gave us both excellent references, which we needed to obtain more work as we were trusted in people's homes. Our place was never to be nosey – discretion was everything.

Chapter 12

Bridget found alternative employment and I went to live-in with the Rapon family in Highgate, almost down the road from my husband-to-be.

What a family they were. This again was a live-in position as a nanny and housekeeper to Mr Edwin Rapon and Mrs Erika Rapon's two children, Clarence and Samantha.

Life was going to change for the better and it was time to settle into my new home. I was going to come into contact with the world of actors, writers, poets and artists. Not forgetting good food, a comfortable home for some years ahead, and a wonderful family to work for. Yes, I can honestly say these were the happiest days of my working life and a second home to Ireland.

Bridget was settled for the time being and so when we got a night off we tried to go to the pictures once a week. We would go to a department store and spray ourselves with perfume testers and wear the same clothes but swap scarves and brooches. We would queue in the rain for a ticket. *High Society* would be showing and we were a couple of wee eejits staring at the screen wishing we could dress like Grace Kelly!

* * *

It transpired that my sister Lily managed to gain some employment in England, through the same agency in Belfast. She came with a friend and they both found domestic live-in positions in the Uxbridge area. She did not stay in the household long before both of them left their respective jobs and got a day job and rented a caravan. Lily found it difficult to conform and did not realise that living in, although with drawbacks, was more secure for a woman on her own.

My mother wrote to me at the Rapon's, forewarning me about Lily coming over to England. She did not want her at home in Ireland and I do not know how she expected me to look after her when I was living-in other people's home. There were no relatives to come to her aid. She needed help to look after the baby and find her a home.

So, when Lily arrived in England she came over to see me in Highgate. It was also a shock to me that she had fallen pregnant in Ireland when she was sixteen to one of local boys. She apparently gave birth to a boy and my mother immediately gave the child to her sister Maggie to rear. The child died within three months and a wee wooden box was made by our brother, Terry. He painted it white and the baby was quietly buried in a cemetery in the Tempo area. Nothing more was said.

She went on to say that mother had kept her inside the house working as she gradually enlarged, and made her was the auld clothes every morning. She was not up to pulling and humping the washing as it was mighty heavy. Confining her gave the neighbours the impression that nothing was wrong. Apparently my father did not have an inkling that she was pregnant until our brother John realised and told our father. *Oh boy*, Lily said, did he give her a *tongue-in* (telling off).

After finding this out, I was so surprised that she should find herself pregnant again. It happened when Lily was working in Belfast where numerous sailors disembarked at the docks. The sailors came off the ships in droves. Men and women were plenty full and the inevitable took its course.

Gradually this second pregnancy started to get a little more noticeable, but she managed to carry on in her day job until it became too much. Then it was left to me to find her a place to be looked after.

She had the baby in a nursing home in Muswell Hill, not far from me. It was Christmas 1946 and I was trying to sort out accommodation.

In the end we had to go to a convent in Highgate for unmarried mothers. The nuns took her in. A film director was interested in adopting the baby boy, but after some consideration she did not want to part with him so Mrs Rapon very kindly let me look after my sister in their home. There was enough room as she could share my room. As there was five years difference and I was the eldest girl I felt a responsibility to look after her.

After giving birth and Lily felt well, Mrs Rapon managed to get her a daily domestic job and rent free room in exchange for housework. This enabled her to take care of her baby and carry out the housework for a lady, Mrs Barnes. Mrs Rapon also provided her with a second-hand cot, pram and baby clothes.

Then in conversation Mrs Barnes mentioned to Mrs Rapon that some of her stockings had gone missing and was accusing my sister of stealing them. If she had, she could well afford them. Again, middle class and mean. It would not have hurt her to be a little generous and give her a packet. But she still kept Lily on.

* * *

Edwin Rapon was involved in the theatre in the 1930s. He had been Principal of the preparatory academy of the Royal Academy of Dramatic Arts, RADA, then based in Shepherd's Hill. Further on in his career he was also Drama Director of the Guildhall of Music and Drama.

He was an approachable, pleasant and very interesting human being and when we had a conversation he would never talk down to me. He worked with theatres throughout the country and gave John Gregson his first part in a play while he was with the Liverpool Playhouse shortly after the Second World War.

In 1943 he was the first to produce a play by the scriptwriter Ted (Lord Willis) titled *Buster*. It starred Alfie Bass, which was also his first role. So he put both these famous actors on the road to fame.

He was very liberal in his political views: well, to be quite frank, he had slight communist tendencies. These came to light when he made a trip to America and was not allowed to enter the United States without in-depth questioning.

Mr Rapon was a student at Cambridge University, where I believe he met his wife, Erika - a scholar who spoke several languages. She came from Berlin I recall. Her father was a German Jew and a communist in Berlin during the Second World War. He was shot by the Gestapo whilst in a German concentration camp. Her mother remained in Berlin and they both visited one another regularly.

Erika's mother had a strong German accent, plaited hair, and she would walk round the flat saying to the children in broken English *"ello our kid"*. She would later send me attractive clothes from Germany for my daughter. Sometimes Erika's sister, Renee, would come and stay.

The Rapons had a large spacious apartment on the Muswell Hill Road, Highgate. The entrance had mahogany, glass swing doors. The hallway was stacked full of book shelves.

Off the main hall to the right was the first bedroom, then the lounge with a baby grand piano. From the lounge straight back into the hallway was another bedroom on the right, another bedroom on the left which was mine, then a small shared bathroom and toilet. Further along was a very small galley kitchen on the left. Straight ahead was the dining-room which overlooked the gardens, lawn and other apartments in the distance.

On the windowsill was displayed a pair of Rudolf Nuyerev's ballet shoes, not forgetting a bust of the famous Spanish painter, Pablo Picasso. The sculpture of the artist's head was quite magnificent, in white papier mache. Where she originally obtained it from, I do not know.

Some years later, during the summer of July and August, Erika was to run The Chelsea Holiday School for foreign students interested in the theatre. My daughter would help out with the booking forms and letters. This she did for a few years and was paid £100 per annum and gave her some pocket money.

They rented their flat, which was quite common in Highgate. Erika educated me in tastes of food, such as Twinings tea, continental biscuits, fresh ground coffee, German cake, chocolates, Tiptree jam and lots of other goodies. The first time I had seen brown sugar was at the Rapons. Erika's clothes were really chic and stylish, always shopped at the best department stores.

I would take the children, Samantha and Clarence, to Fortnum and Mason for afternoon tea, which was a sheer delight. Just the three of us.

Erika believed in living and experiencing. She missed her continental upbringing. When she returned from Germany she would say to me: "*Oh Mary, I get so depressed coming back here."* It was not the climate she was referring to I think, but just living a different way of life, and memories of her father triggered off these feelings.

Although terrifically good natured, Erika could never manage to pay my wages on time. When I did eventually get them I managed to save some money. She just would forget. Because she travelled abroad so much and appeared restless she relied on me to keep the home running and I became a part of the family. She mentioned that she wanted to become an actress but her ambition did not come to fruition. Maybe another person inside her wanted to be released.

When Samantha reached eighteen years of age she decided to study languages, especially Russian, at University. At one stage I saw her on the credits of a wine programme in the 1980s.

Clarence studied music and his forte was the cello, which he played in the London production of *The Taste of Honey*. He was a darling little boy and was always hungry. After school he would go into the kitchen and take a slice of brown bread and cover it with a nob of butter and honey – straight into his mouth in one go. His mother told me that when he was a little boy she had a feeling that he would grow up a homosexual, not that she objected as she moved in those circles all the time. She had a close friend, Christian, whom I met on numerous occasions at some of Rapon's soirées, who was partial to wearing a little make-up of face powder, rouge for cheek colour and a final touch of lipstick - outrageous then but acceptable now.

Later my daughter and I were so lucky as I invariably got free tickets from Mrs Rapon to go to the theatre to see Rex Harrison in *My Fair Lady,* where we sat in the stalls. During the interval we had tea and biscuits served on a tray, brought to us in our seats.

Mrs Rapon knew so many people that sometimes I did know the names of the people staying. She flew home once with a pilot who, on board his plane, carried mink pelts so as to have a coat made up. She helped many people with accommodation, food and even money.

A time comes to mind when Mr Rapon's brother, Charles, had been invited to dinner with his wife and Erika asked me to cook a chicken. She disappeared to town in central London for some reason and later telephoned me to say that she was not feeling too well and was not returning home that night. She had probably met someone and decided to stay the night with them - a practice not uncommon. I used to put this action down to feeling low.

Charles Rapon was in the Air Force and married twice. His first marriage was to the proprietor's daughter of the well-known department store, *Gamages*. I heard she left Charles Rapon for Roy Boulting, the film director, and then left him for a

French film director.

I can recall one miserable foggy day when I returned home to find Erika in the kitchen. The gas oven was on and she was on her knees bending over trying to gas herself. Thanks be to God I found her in time.

I put this incident down to suffering with her nerves and it could be related to the traumatic death of her poor father.

Chapter 13

Edwin Rapon had a book published in 1963 called *Drama as a Career*. On the front cover was a photograph of a young, handsome Peter O'Toole giving advice to a drama student (Samantha posing for the photograph only). Because of his interesting profession, it enabled Mr Rapon to come into contact with so many up-and-coming people who are still famous today. They frequented at the Rapon's home often.

Michael Dennison and Dulcie Gray got together when she attended the Webber Douglas Drama School. One of their films called *The Glass Mountain* was made in 1945. I absolutely adored the film – the music always stuck in my mind. When Michael Dennison came visiting he always looked elegant and charming, epitomising the English gentleman. Another frequent visitor was the actress Pat Kirkwood who sang the famous song *After the Ball is Over*.

Though I had never met Joan Plowright, actress and wife to Sir Laurence Olivier, she visited the Rapons on occasion and made her theatre debut at The Old Vic in 1951. She married Sir Laurence Olivier in 1961. Mrs Rapon said that when she first met Joan there was something about her that she took an instant dislike to. Being a great fan of Vivien Leigh, she could not imagine Olivier with *her*.

Patrick Hamilton - renowned for writing the famous Victorian thriller stage play *Gaslight* in 1938 and the novel *Hangover Square* in 1941 - would often telephone the flat and he and I would have a chat. He asked me out several times, when phoning, but I always declined owing to his reputation. Mrs Rapon told me he was in the process of having an affair with a prostitute and she was pregnant. What happened to the child I never found out. He liked a drink or two.

Whenever he came to the door I had the pleasure of greeting him. He was polite and well-mannered with a rounded face and brown rimmed spectacles, an aura of intelligentsia sorrounding him. He died in 1962.

Around February 1948 I was still living-in but I would still carry on working for the Rapons. Clarence was lucky enough to obtain an acting part playing a small boy called *Finn* in the play *Silver Darling*. He was acting with Robert Newton, who at the time was playing Bill Sykes in *Oliver Twist*.

The studio's chauffeur dropped Robert Newton off at the flat and took Clarence and I to Golders Green to buy him a pair of shoes to go to the studio with. After shopping we returned home and Newton and Clarence went to the studio to rehearse.

Mr Newton had a reputation amongst the acting fraternity of never being sober. Whenever I saw him at the flat you could tell he had been drinking. When in conversation with him about his part in *Oliver,* he said that once, when he was inebriated, he clouted his wife over the head with the telephone receiver. Maybe he was playing a part.

* * *

North London seemed to attract many up-and-coming actors and one in particular was the wonderful Peter O'Toole, who won a scholarship to RADA. I said hello to him when he came to the flat and I thought how good looking he was. In later life his profession would take him to higher levels. He married the actress Sian Phillips and lived not far from Dudley Moore and Suzy Kendall. When I lived in North Finchley I often went to Hampstead and passed his house in Heath Street.

There was always such a mixture of talent and personalities arriving at Rapons. I suppose it could not be helped given his profession.

The great ballet dancer, Rudolf Nureyev, passed through also. He was very much on Mrs Rapon's mind. I know she had a brief affair with him. Who could not love Nureyev! The ballet shoes belonging to him, displayed on the dining-room windowsill, showing his written signature on the soles, is still immersed in my memory.

The Rapons were always being invited to first nights at the theatre. On one occasion Mrs Rapon had just returned to the flat late, and told me that they had just been to a gathering with Peter O'Toole and Rudolf Nureyev adding to the guest list. The two men were chatting and being silly and the next thing Rudolf Nureyev threw Peter O'Toole over his shoulder and hastily went off into one of the bedrooms. Perhaps the drink had got to them!

* * *

How lucky can one get to come into contact with Dylan Thomas, that wonderful Welsh writer and poet? With his dishevelled hair and striking Welsh accent, down to earth and easy to get along with – a terrific drinker and smoker who often came to visit.

It was around May 1953 and the world premiere of Dylan Thomas' play *Under Milk Wood*, with Thomas playing the part of the narrator. It was being shown in New York and he had go over there to see the Assistant Director. He was en-route to America via Highgate, flying out from Heathrow Airport. I had the pleasure of ironing a shirt for him. I wish, now, I had framed it!

The love affair was short, and Erika fell for his Welsh charm. All women adored him. This time it was serious, and she became pregnant. It led to her having an abortion, almost causing her death and had an abortion and almost died in the process. I visited her in hospital and looked after her when she was discharged.

Jonathan Miller and John McGrath were two very interesting young people. Miller was an author, with many other attributes. But he was very young then and so was everyone else. John McGrath, whom the young Samantha had a crush on as she was growing up, helped shape a generation of Scottish Theatre during his career. He died aged sixty-six with leukaemia (the same disease as my brother Mickey who died aged fifty-two).

Because Erika Rapon loved and admired the arts so much she visited the theatre often, especially on the first night, standing outside by the stage door until she managed to greet her idols and ask them for an autograph. Normally she had seats for the first night. When Tennessee Williams' book *A Street Car Named Desire* became popular and a play written, Erika went along to watch it and waited with baited breath until she managed to ask him for his autograph. Earlier in the evening he was sitting in the audience for the first night so she seized the opportunity.

All these people enhanced lives - not only for the Rapons, but for me and many others.

Chapter 14

By this time Lily was still living in a room and working as a daily domestic. We were close to one another and we could both keep an eye on James, her son.

It was winter and the two of us were walking in Highgate Woods when two young men stopped us. For a little light relief we began talking, whilst James was sleeping in his pram. They were now civilians free to do what they liked. People were friendlier then after being discharged - the war was over.

One of the men, Edward, invited me for a drink that evening as Lily had to get home with James. We arranged to meet at the Woodman Pub, Highgate. That evening Edward asked me out again but insisted I bring Lily next time so we could make a foursome with his brother Victor. So we had to find Lily a babysitter for the following evening. Bridget would oblige. I waited for Lily to turn up and we had a great night laughing about anything and everything.

Neither of us wanted to stay out late as it was unacceptable to our employers. Lily had to get home to her baby and Bridget had promised to babysit for a couple of hours only. We all arranged to meet up at the same place, but this time with his brother, Victor.

Edward fell for Lily - I fell for Victor. He looked like a gentleman to me. Gentle, handsome and quiet - with blue eyes, brown receding hair, and a clear complexion. I was hooked! I had already made up my mind that I would never marry an Irish man, for in my opinion they drank too much.

During the war Victor was in the Royal Marines. The exact title was RM Driver (Landing Craft) from June 1944 to June 1945. Enlistment was on 12th October 1943. He was stationed in Ceylon and Egypt, as well as various places in England. He lived with his mother, Hetty Kate Emily, father Albert, and his brothers - Albert, Cliff, Ronald, Edward, Leonard - and one sister, Doreen. There were two other children in the family but they died from neglect. Even Victor had to be checked because of malnutrition.

They started life in a council flat on Summbersby Road, Highgate. When my in-laws were older the council moved them to a small one bedroomed bungalow off Fortis Green Road where mother-in-law was to come into contact with the mother of Ray Davis, of the Kinks pop group, who lived just around the corner and was always wearing her slippers.

Victor's brother, Ronald, would send letters home to their mother until the day came when she received a telegram that he had been killed in action and was buried in Caen, Normandy. In years to come, Doreen gave these to Victor to keep.

Edward on the other hand was stationed at Monte Cassino Monastery in Italy that had been bombarded by the German in 1944. He was shot twice in the army but managed to survive.

So in 1946 they decided to get married and set a

wedding date. They also put their name down on the housing list as soon as possible. Edward would now be my sister's husband and her baby's adopted father. It did not take them long to obtain a council flat and they moved to Finsbury Park. Doreen helped furnish it and made curtains and the boys painted and decorated – we all helped out.

It was difficult to have a relationship living in someone else's home and there was no money to throw around so we had to go somewhere. One night Victor came back to the Rapons for a cup of tea and stayed until three o'clock in the morning. So it was around January 1948 when I found myself pregnant. It was another shock and he was the first man I had been intimate with. Victor's mother was not happy and accused me of keeping her son out until the early hours of the morning. There was no doubt in my mind that I wanted to marry Victor.

Victor and I courted for six months of knowing each other. As for my other boyfriend, Prince – well, he did not seem to take the news too badly and, after all, the relationship was spasmodic. I had been seeing Prince for five years and he came from Shropshire. If he wanted to marry me he should have hurried up and got on with a proposal!

During my time off me and Victor went to the pictures, nicknamed the Flea Pit, in East Finchley. It was a bit of a dump and shabby looking but was all we could afford on Victor's wages. We always went to the evening programme and sat in the back row holding hands and smoking. We so looked forward to being together and having a cigarette - watching *Gone with the Wind, Singing in the Rain* and the great John Wayne westerns.

Vic always mimicked him; the title of the film has slipped my mind right now. But I will never forget Clark Gable and Vivien Leigh in her southern bell dresses. There were films like *A Kid for two Farthings* starring Diana Dors and *The Third Man,* starring the wonderful Orson Wells. They were great films. Rock 'n' Roll was not widely heard of in England in 1956 but later to follow were a pair of teenagers named John Lennon and Paul McCartney.

Times were changing.

We married on the eighth of May 1949 at the Registry Office in the District of Wood Green in the county of Middlesex, the day before his twenty-second birthday.

We celebrated by going to the pictures to see the film *The Red Shoes* with Moira Shearer: a romantic film about a ballerina torn between love for her husband and her love for dancing. At the end of the film she goes on stage but then changes her mind and gives up her dancing to be with her husband. Ever since then I have a fondness for the film. And as I love the colour red, I even managed to buy a pair of red high-heel open toed shoes which, I treasured and wore threadbare.

I gave birth to my daughter on twentieth October 1948 and she weighed eight and a half pounds. The nurses at the Nursing Home in Muswell Hill (the same one as my sister Lily) commented on Jackie's bone structure, especially her legs. Later her grandfather was to call her *The Tiller Girl* from the London Palladium, because of her long legs.

So we started our married life with my in-laws for two years in Highgate. We needed somewhere to live for the time being. Ten of us in a small flat, we would talk about having our own home, but it was a long way off.

I always found my mother-in-law financially mean and hard. She showed this side when, one winter morning, I cooked a couple of slices of bacon and my mother-in-law asked me to pay for them. Another time she was on the bus with my daughter and asked her for the fare. When I tried to find a cotton dress belonging to my daughter it was filthy as she had cleaned the fire grate with it.

We were just getting on our feet as Victor was an apprentice learning plumbing and central heating. This took five years to complete so my wages were to come in useful and we wanted to save. His mother was disciplined and her family always had breakfast, lunch, dinner, and supper. At bedtime they would all have a hot drink. She did her best I suppose.

Hetty Kate Emily had a job working as a cleaner for a doctor, which was a godsend: one day she noticed some blood oozing from her right nipple and she mentioned it to her employer. The doctor referred her to another doctor, who diagnosed breast cancer. Immediately she had a breast removed. (My daughter was to have breast cancer, also in the nipple and would have her breast removed.)

Unlike today, where we have modern prosthetics, my mother-in-law had to make do with birdseed packs, which took the place of her original breast. I never heard her complain whilst skivvying, although my father-in-law was known to be lazy and work shy. Being in the First World War may account for his lack of enthusiasm for work as he did lose some of his hearing during the bombing and blasting.

* * *

My daughter was just six week's old when I found a domestic position with Olive and Irene Pound. The two spinsters lived in Highgate together, so they were quite local. This position was purely cleaning and my husband and I desperately needed the money.

I commenced work at eight o'clock in the morning and had a break - yes a break! - at ten o'clock. Olive gave me a slice of bread with jam and I sat in the kitchen with a cup of tea.

I would prepare their lunch for twelve noon, before going back to my mother-in-law's flat to take over from her as she was looking after my daughter until midday. I never had time for lunch or any kind of break apart from ten o'clock. They wanted me to work Saturday mornings as well to do a few hours.

Their surname was unusual at the time, but that could not compare to their meanness when paying me. They should have been called Olive and Irene shillings, or even pennies!

Despite this, Olive and I had a good rapport. She had been employed in the civil service, which was quite something in those days. As for Irene, she worked as a housekeeper - a level up from me working in a much larger household with staff under her. I referred to her as the *auld cow,* which is putting it mildly. I would know my place: she had a stern Victorian voice probably resulting in their upbringing as their brother was a judge by profession.

When it came to cleaning their flat – boy, did they teach me how to clean! In fact they taught me using a chamois leather and vinegar to wipe their antique furniture every three months. After cleaning the complete bathroom suite, taps had to be polished off with a dry cloth. In the kitchen, on my knees, I scrubbed the kitchen floor without leaving a speck of dust. Irene would give me a demonstration, and I would be asked to clean it all again, then she would inspect it.

One morning Olive Pound said she thought I looked rather pale and withdrawn so she made me drink a pint of milk to build up my calcium intake. They could starve a mouse out of a hole with their carefulness with money but the milk suggestion was kind and considerate.

On this particular morning, whilst scrubbing the

floors, I had an aching head and was not feeling too well. This was beginning to affect my work so I visited the doctor. It was found to be sinusitis.

So I had to go to hospital for eight appointments to have my sinuses scraped, which involved a long metal "needle" being put up each nostril. It was so painful that I could not bear to keep the last appointment. I have never had a problem since.

After finishing with the Pound's job in the morning, I would return home to my mother-in-law and daughter and take over by feeding and changing her nappy. Changing nappies would mean soaking them in cold water, then boiling them as they were made out of heavy towelling. My mother-in-law would return home at two o'clock and I would go to the Rapons in order to do a few hours. We managed between us to keep this routine up for a couple of years.

At Christmas the Pounds gave me one pound for a present. *Wasn't I lucky!* No wonder they could afford to leave one hundred and thirty-five thousand pounds in their will to their brother who was the sole beneficiary. Irene was the first to pass away, followed by dear Olive.

My wages earned me two pound ten shillings a week, along with other jobs. Out of this I had to pay my mother-in-law thirty shillings, which included all our accommodation. The remainder went on our food.

Victor was on his apprenticeship so he was not earning very much, but we managed until he would qualify as a plumber and heating engineer.

* * *

It was coming to a time that after two years of living with my in-laws, we needed to be on our own. We walked the feet off ourselves trying to find accommodation that would take a two-year-old child. Eventually we found a landlady in Muswell Hill, who was willing to rent out a large room to us, sharing the bathroom and toilet which was on the landing. I was worried about the other tenants and she said: *"if they do not like the sound of a child crying then they will have to put cotton wool in their ears!"*

Our prayers were answered and we were to stay here for the next four years.

We had our fair share of problems and had to watch our money with the gas and electricity meter by putting shillings in the slots. We would both wash in the sink and Jackie would have a bowl in front of the fire where her father would bathe her.

Victor was patient and helpful with our daughter. Mrs Rapon also allowed me to bring Jackie to the flat when she was not at nursery school, only I had to be careful that she did not touch their grand piano or Samantha's dolls house

I continued working for the Rapons and was recommended to work for a Mrs Pierson whose apartment was situated on the opposite side from the Rapons, across the lawns. Good nannies and domestic staff were still sought after, even though there were plenty to go around. Employers always preferred recommendations and Irish girls were extremely popular and reliable because they had travelled a long way from home, were from poor families, and grateful to work.

Chapter 15

Mrs Pierson came from a middle class family and was working as an actress, which also involved her in radio programmes. She had a delightful, distinctive husky voice and in looks was slim and attractive. When listening to her voice on the radio your ears pricked up – you could tell it was her by the deep huskiness and gravelly throaty voice. I heard her on the radio programme when she took part in the *Scarlet Pimpernel.* She also acted in several stage plays and was an understudy to Hermione Gingold. I had the pleasure of going to the theatre and seeing her act one time.

She had a son called Lance, who was a bonnie boy. Apart from taking care of Lance, I also did the usual housework and ironing. Lance went on to be educated at Eton then Oxford. I keep a black and white photograph of him taken in 1952 still in the family photograph album. She especially asked me to iron Lance's silk romper suits that were hand-made and were a real effort to press because they were flimsy and fiddly, especially the buttonholes.

Her apartment was the exact size of the Rapons'. Sometimes her mother would come and visit. She had one sister who was a doctor and a divorcee.

Mrs Pierson never arose before eleven in the morning. When she saw me buzzing around the flat she had a tendency to ignore me completely as if I were invisible, until she had her first cup of coffee. She was always moody first thing. I learned to ignore the mornings and let her have her coffee.

I enjoyed working for her and looking after Lance. My own daughter was now at the Whittingham Preparatory School in Muswell Hill so this enabled my husband and me to earn some money for our rent and also pay for her to go to nursery school. My mother-in-law would collect her and look after her until I went to pick her up, so I could be flexible in my hours.

Mrs Pierson was to be our saviour when it was time to purchase our first home by offering us a loan to help with the mortgage. But this was still to come in a few years' time.

Some Sundays, as a family day out, we would take a blanket and some sandwiches and go with my in-laws to Alexandra Palace, *Ally Pally,* overlooking the superb views above London.

Then one damp, foggy cold winter's morning my husband took a bad cold. I called in to the doctor and he diagnosed bronchitis. That night my husband woke me in the middle of the night as he was burning a fever, and perspiring profusely. I applied a cold face flannel to his forehead until I managed to go round to the doctor in the morning. He gave us a home visit and administered some penicillin as the infection had turned to pleurisy. He could not continue working and had to stay at home for three months.

My daughter was two years and ten months, getting on for nearly three. I kept her home from nursery school because she kept her father busy throwing balls backwards and forwards - amusing one another and passing the time.

I would depart from the bedsit at seven-thirty in the morning to catch the bus to Shepherd's Hill, Highgate so I could walk down to my first job to clean for a woman who had two children doing domestic duties. The mean auld bastards paid me half-a-crown for three hours work.

Then on to the Rapons, then to my other employer, Mrs Pierson. When I had finished by one o'clock I would go home to get lunch and would get the bus back to Highgate to finish my other jobs.

Sometimes the Rapons would ask me to clean the Royal Academy of Arts, round and about but not often. I had four or five jobs on the go. Thank God I was healthy.

Life continued this way and I was always working for the Rapons and Mrs Pierson until Jackie was ready to go St Michael's Convent in Muswell Hill, where I had to pay for her private school fees.

The convent is where I met the mother of one of Jackie's friends, Barbara Farrant. She was married to Donald Ferrant, who I believe went to Sandhurst and had been a Major in the army. He was in business and owned his own factory, so was quite comfortable. She had two children: Valerie, whom Jackie went to school with, and a son called David.

Barbara lived with her family in a large Victorian house in Shepherd's Hill. Their house was just opposite where the Beverly Sisters' lived and later Peter Sellers' resided nearby and so did many of the acting fraternity.

She was a nurse at St. Bartholomew's Hospital. With her long blond hair and slim elegant figure, she would stand out in a crowd. For a change she and I would go out for a night to the pictures. She also liked Chinese food, so when it was her birthday we would go into town, heading for Tottenham Court Road on the tube and dine at Freddie Mill's - the boxer's Chinese restaurant. Alas, we did not get even a glimpse of the famous pugilist, but we enjoyed the meal.

After a visit to her doctor for a check-up, Barbara received some devastating news. She was referred to the hospital for an X-ray. There was no such machine as a CT scanner then, but a tumour on the brain was discovered. Soon after she died. She was only thirty-two.

I missed her cheerful smile – she had been such fun. It was a terrible loss to Don and her two children. I assume that she was buried in Highgate cemetery.

Some years on, when my family were visiting Edward in Finsbury Park, I read an article about a grave that had been desecrated by a young man named David Farrant. I could only infer from this that the grave may have belonged to his mother. The News of the World also picked up a story and it made centre page; that a man called David Farrant had been practising witchcraft and had been taking drugs. I also read that he had been imprisoned for about five years. He was accused of taking a one-hundred-year corpse from Highgate cemetery.

Chapter 16

In 1954 we took advantage of Mrs Pierson's offer to accept a loan. We had saved a little money and Victor was now a qualified tradesman earning six pound ten shillings a week. We had opened up a joint Lloyds bank account so that we could pay our bills into a Post Office savings book.

We could not afford to buy a house in North London, as we would have liked, but I was determined to move back there in the coming future when we could afford it. So we purchased our first end terrace: a three-bedroom house with a medium sized garden, which needed work, and an alleyway running down the side of it. This was Southall in Middlesex. As my husband was a practical man the house itself would need decorating and a new garden but not much more.

Jackie was moved from her school so we had to find her an alternative. Victor acquired a second-hand green bicycle that transported him to work and back. Depending on where he was working, he would take pity on some of the animals and pets he would come across. Once he brought home two white doves, a rabbit, a budgerigar and a "tabby" kitten which we kept named Wobby Willie - nicknamed because his mother had lain on his right back leg as a kitten and when he walked he was like hop-along Cassidy.

The next purchase was a television - a brown

square box with a small screen. You had to fiddle with the aerial to get a reasonable black and white picture. The 1950s also brought us programmes like Dixon of Dock Green and Dragnet. So we would settle down on a Saturday evening to watch Juke Box Jury and we would eat beans on toast on a tray on our laps.

Still getting a haphazard picture from the screen, my husband would spend time moving the aerial around and we would live in hope for an evening's viewing. A great entertainment for the working classes.

On Sunday afternoons our neighbours would invite other neighbours children into their home from around the area, for tea and to watch Liberace, the American pianist.

Jackie was around seven years old now. We were settling into our first home. I kept in touch with the Rapons occasionally at Christmas, but never saw them until we returned to North London, so I had to find some new employers whilst living in Middlesex. We were still budgeting and scouting the second hand shops to buy furniture that we could paint.

So I looked around for work in Hanger Lane and noticed the area was not as affluent as north London. Still, luck was on my side and I found a job looking after a little baby girl, the dog, and some light cleaning work.

The Brombergs were an American Jewish family

living in Greystoke Court, Hanger Lane. Mr Bromberg was a pilot at the Ruislip American base. The dog's name was Pretzels and was a sandy coloured terrier, whippet cross. The pay was good and I liked the family.

Pretzels would greet me at the door when I arrived at the flat, then she would pick up the baby's toys and drop them at her tiny feet and tilt her head. When it was time to leave, Pretzels would see me off by barking goodbye. I worked for them practically every day until they went back to America. When they went back home for a holiday, they would leave Pretzels with us. But when they returned for good – we kept Pretzels. Now we had two pets, a cat and dog.

My name was passed on to another American family, the Bottomleys. They were Jewish too and her husband worked at the Ruislip American base, also as a pilot. They were good payers as well.

Mrs Bottomley told me that her niece had married Rex Harrison, the actor, but as he married six times, I cannot remember the niece's name. They had two very young children and a dog. No, we did not need another one!

One Christmas we were invited to a party. Victor, not being a drinker, had one drink, then another, until someone mixed his drinks and he was violently sick. We had to leave him there, slumped over the toilet pan. Mr Bottomley brought him back the following morning, his skin looking grey. This would put him off alcohol in future.

For Christmas presents Mrs Bottomley gave my daughter an America doll with knitted dresses and cardigans in a variety of colours and a ranch similar to a doll's house. At the same time Victor had walked three miles to collect a shiny black doll's pram, which he had to hide under a white sheet on Christmas Eve for Jackie.

My husband was rather work-shy and his family said he took after his father. He was a quiet person and did not like to mix with people, preferring to work on his own. He was happy decorating and renovating the house. There were bouts of him not being interested in finding work and he was always a worrier, which contributed to his lack of confidence. His wetting the bed at the beginning of our marriage was a cause for concern, but slowly he improved and the problem subsided.

At times I thought about leaving him. I was worried about paying the bills and he would take money out of my purse, thinking I was unaware of what was going on. I would put as much money as I could into the joint bank account - but when it came to paying some bills, the money disappeared. He was putting less and less in the account, only enough to pay for the monthly mortgage payments and rates, but often that would diminish I just assumed he was going to his work for a full day.

I felt this could not go on and I took the initiative

of opening my own post office savings account, not telling him, and kept it a secret. The book was hidden in the bottom of my large handbag, together with my make-up and cigarettes, and I carried it everywhere.

We had a child, giving us more responsibility, and I had a fear of not being able to manage. At least he did the decorating and gardening and I was happy with that.

He could be unreliable and have black mood swings. Perhaps this was a result of the war and being the first person to come off a landing craft to see the devastation of bodies displayed in front of him. But I needed someone and I certainly did not want an actual divorce, being a Catholic, although the possibility did cross my mind at times.

Working hard, cleaning up other people's homes, I just had enough energy left to clean mine.

* * *

After giving birth to James in 1946 Lily broke the news that she had fallen pregnant for the third time and decided to go home to Ireland for her annual holiday with him. The local people were so bigoted and narrow minded that she was frightened to mention the connection. She led the neighbours to think he belonged to her sister-in-law, Doreen, and that she was bringing him home for a holiday; you could see the McCann Irish resemblance.

In October 1948, the year Jackie was born, she

gave birth to her third son: Robert. The child was born in the Erne Hospital in Ireland. From thereon Lily would always spend six weeks every year going home to Ireland, which caused homesickness every time she returned to England.

* * *

Everyone was in the same situation with finding work in Northern Ireland, which was so scarce. So we ended up with a few visitors: my brothers would alternate to stay with us for six months, mainly just to get some money together and take home to Ireland. Terry first, then Mickey and John. All three came and went but Seamus and Charlie came to England and stayed.

Seamus was nineteen, very shy, with a turn in his eye. When he arrived he decided to stay after meeting his future wife, June. They had very little money so they had their wedding reception at our house. I supplied the food and the party was in full swing. June's uncle provided the entertainment and proceeded to pass his hat around for a collection.

Seamus had various jobs and eventually was employed by the Electricity Board. Sadly he died aged fifty-six in 1993, of a tumour on the brain. Two colleagues also died of the same illness. The Union began looking into this problem. His wife had breast cancer earlier on in their marriage and then had ovarian cancer, despite having bouts of chemotherapy. Through all her suffering she was to die seven years after my brother Seamus.

In between the family, we also had Joe McCaffrey lodge with us for a time. He suffered depression and late one evening I went into his bedroom and found him lying on the floor. He slept there all night and he did this every night. His brother was a priest and somehow I felt he would be better at home with his own people, not at Rutland Road. The rent he paid came in handy when he was working, but I did not relish the thought of having a lodger under my roof with mental health problems. He soon came to his senses and returned home to Ireland to his family.

Time passed by continuing with the family comings and goings until Charlie, my youngest brother, arrived on the scene. Trouble was coming our way. He was the last of us twelve children. What a time we had with him! The wild man from Borneo, fresh from the country.

He was wild, impulsive, young and out of control. He was just twenty-two, with little education. He was used to running the roads in Ireland with no responsibility and no parental control. He was a likeable tearaway then and put roots down with us for a time. But the drinking and the drugs became a real problem, as well as the company he used to keep - mainly petty criminals.

Every night he would come home late and the

alcohol made him aggressive. He would push my husband up against the wall and grab his neck and threaten him. When he was sober he was gentle.

After earning some money on the buildings he purchased a "Consul" saloon car on hire purchase. Victor acted as a guarantor for the hire purchase agreement. Charlie, however, was incapable of keeping to his side of the bargain and defaulted with the payments. My husband was taken to court and made to take over the monthly repayments.

Because Charlie was my brother I felt responsible for him, so I repaid the loan for my husband. Charlie could be as mad as a hatter and would drive the car without his hands on the steering wheel, freewheeling.

A girlfriend came along to take his mind off his mad antics and he moved to North London to stay with my sister Lily for a while. His lady friend already had three children from her first relationship and, whilst he had a spell at Her Majesty's Service, he married her in prison.

Charlie always lived for the moment. When he was discharged from prison we very rarely saw him – and did not want to. Trouble was his middle name. There was something bothering him throughout his adult life.

My parents were glad to see the back of him in Ireland and none of my sisters wanted him to return. We hoped marriage would settle him down, and they had three more lovely girls. The drinking, drugs and criminal activity did not change and after thirty years of marriage his wife left him.

Not long after the separation, in November 1999, he had a sudden heart attack and died – aged 58. *At least he found some peace.* To be fair to my husband, with all my family coming from Ireland and staying with us, he was very tolerant and never complained, even when he was being *strangled!* In general the Swannell family gave us no trouble whatsoever in our marriage - it was the McCann clan.

* * *

After riding a bike to and from work my husband needed a van to transport his tools in, so he bought his first vehicle - an A30 Austin van. It was in a very poor state of repair, but road worthy for those days. He parked it at the back of the garden, behind the fence, as we had no garage. It needed spraying and some fibre glass repair to fill in the holes and rusted parts. So he saved the newspapers and covered the whole vehicle with the sheets and purchased a spray gun and sprayed the van dark blue. He also reinforced the floor.

He drove around in the van with learner L plates but never took his test for a year. When he did, he passed first time. It was goodbye to bike and hello to van.

He was getting some more work with having the van; I was cleaning at Hanger Lane; Jackie was at school. We were going up in the world!

Every year I gave my daughter a birthday party in October and she would design her own party dress and choose the material. The dressmaker would make up the dress, which was always beautiful. Victor would sort out some games for the children like *pin the tail on the donkey.*

My nephews would often stay with us and take the long bus ride over to Rutland Road, which meant more mouths to feed.

After some distance between the two boys, Lily was expecting her fourth boy, Simon. So the two boys would come over to me whilst she was coping at home for her new arrival. The marriage was somewhat strained, and she had a brief affair with a man who owned a tobacconist shop close to her home. She regretted the affair but not having her son. Now she had three boys to contend with.

Chapter 17

Around 1958, after four years of living in Southall, we were looking for our second home.

We saw a house that we liked, but we could not afford the mortgage. So the estate agent wrote to the mortgage company stating that my husband was earning more and we got our mortgage. Our second home was in sight. It was similar to our last home but was a larger terraced house, with a garage and a very large garden in a tree-lined avenue.

We had to get Jackie settled into a new school and our life would now settle down at last.

I managed to keep up my visits to Ireland. One year we took Samantha Rapon with us for a week's holiday, as I was working for Rapons again - just a few days a week until I found a job with more hours.

I finally managed to secure a position working for a Professor of Zoology and his wife, a college lecturer, Doctor Terry, looking after the house and taking care of their two children five days a week. It was a full-time job.

I had to get to Whetstone where they lived, take them to school, and return to the house, which was always cold. Doctor Terry would leave me some lunch in the kitchen. In the school holidays, when she was not teaching, I had six weeks off work with pay. I stayed with her for six years, but had to leave in the end as I could not take the cold house, with no heating on in the winter months.

Further along the road lived an Irish lady, whose cousins were the Bachelors, a very famous Irish group. On my way home we would have a chat if I bumped into her and she would tell me the latest news on where they were performing next. My generation really liked them.

One day, reading through the newspaper, I saw in the Situations Vacant column a Jewish family were in need of a nanny. They wanted someone to collect their two girls from school every day and keep the dog company. Both parents were in the retail business, selling mainly male and female jumpers. Sometimes I would babysit on a Saturday evening for extra money and they paid generously, with a box of expensive chocolates to go with it.

But I was tired of looking after children and felt now that I wanted a change.

Work, children and home took over my life. It did not occur to me that my husband had been to see a solicitor about getting a divorce.

I received the letter suggesting that we see a Marriage Guidance Counsellor. Firstly I burst out laughing, then the shock sunk in. We discussed our problems, including the intimate side, and the financial side. As I was working full-time and babysitting in the evening and working Saturdays, some of the money was going to a new Vauxhall Viva car that he was now driving. The intimate side lost its way. Sex for him, money for me.

I felt I had lost respect for him as he was not always looking for work. He would leave the house in the morning and park the car round a side road. As soon as I had left, he would come home and I would not see him until I had finished work and my daughter was home from school.

After this episode with the Marriage Guidance Counsellor, which I refused to attend for even one session, all was calm.

* * *

The 1960s brought many changes. Harold Wilson was the Labour Prime Minister and there was the assassination of President JF Kennedy, the first Irish Catholic President of the United States. I was working at the Orange Tree then and the terrible news left us all dumbfounded and in tears.

As a change, and for less responsibility, I answered an advertisement in the local paper for a Kitchen Assistant to the Chef. I worked at The Orange Tree, a small pub with a silver service restaurant, assisting in the day-to-day running.

The Orange Tree was situated in Totteridge Lane, an affluent part of North London. It was frequented by many celebrities who lived around the area. Charringtons Group owned the pub, but it was leased to a Landlord, who in turn employed an Irish manager and his wife. It was efficiently run and took a good income, becoming incredibly prosperous. The pub itself was old and set back off the road. There was a pond in the front where you had to be careful, as the resident geese could take a notion and attack you.

Gerry, the Chef, and I had some really good laughs. One occasion the waitress had taken an order for an Entrecôte steak, medium rare. So be it.

The customer returned it to the kitchen saying it was under-done. Gerry was stressed as he was the only person cooking. He threw it on the floor, picked it up, flung it into the pan, overcooked it and sent it back with the waitress. Nothing was said by the customer. He was not in a good mood that lunchtime.

He always had a pint on the side and, like most Chefs, was a bit of a drinker - cooking was thirsty work.

I was asked to serve the public once behind the bar as we were short staffed, but I felt more comfortable in the kitchen. Taking and handling money worried me as I would get flustered whilst people were watching me.

Usually I started work at nine thirty in the morning and finished at three o'clock, preparing side salads, prawn cocktails, avocado and prawns (which were popular then). My *piece de resistance* was my Bramley apple pies. Because of my cold hands I would use flour, margarine, eggs and little water. I received nice comments from the regular customers who came in looking for 'Mary's Apple Pie.

There were very few bar staff that lived in but one was a real character. An attractive barman, a fruit merchant (homosexual in Irish words) - which is the name I learned when I was growing up in the country. He would often explain his sexual exploits to me. He was always visiting the doctor owing to back passage problems.

* * *

It was always nice to have a visit from Cliff Richard; he would put his head around the kitchen window to thank Gerry for a tasty delicious curry. He was a regular customer and never failed to acknowledge Gerry or me.

The Shadows, Cliff Richard's backing group, were also regular customers. Hank Marvin came unstuck when trying to read and pronounce the names on the wine list. He usually pointed to his choice of wine to make the waitress understand.

Another customer was the actor Patrick McGoohan, from the TV series *The Prisoner*. He normally came on a Saturday morning for a gin and tonic, never looking right or left but keeping his head down. He would be off after a quick drink.

Des O'Connor and Bruce Forsyth also visited the pub. Des was always subdued and unassuming.

Gossip was always top of the kitchen list. One Christmas Day Anthea Redfern, who was then Bruce Forsyth's glamorous assistant on the TV game show,

The Generation Game, had telephoned him at home and his wife answered. Later, he left his wife for her. So the gossip went. Another time Anne Sydney, who was crowned Miss World, came to the Orange Tree to find out where Bruce Forsyth lived. He was a very popular man.

The singer Frankie Vaughan lived up the road and was always involved in charity work. A well respected happy family man. His home was near the Totteridge Lane Golf Club and he wanted to become a member but he was refused on the grounds of his religion – they did not allow Jews into the club. Hopefully the rules have changed now, but there was a stigma at one time.

Once the Beverley Sisters came in, as they were house hunting for their mother. One would come to the Orange Tree at lunchtime to have a snack. I cannot recall which Beverley sister it was now.

Hattie Jacques was another person coming into the Orange Tree but I never had the pleasure of seeing her in the restaurant. Joe Brown, the guitarist, was another customer.

The actor Ian Carmichael lived up the lane.

We also had a visit from Lord Longford, who wrote a book entitled "Lord Longford on Kennedy", published in 1978.

* * *

The sixties also brought us films starring Sean

Connery and Barbara Windsor, along with the Carry On series. They were exciting, hopeful times. Opportunities for further education, university and better employment choices for young people were in the offing.

I always took the bus home and sometimes I would get a lift. On one occasion I looked out of the kitchen window and saw this two-toned black and yellow Rolls-Royce. I was aghast as I saw my daughter and nephew sitting in the front seat. David Bailey, a well-known fashion photographer, had allowed my nephew to drive it and come and pick me up from work.

Whilst at the Orange Tree I made a variety of acquaintances; one lady working there as a waitress went on to have a career as a dancer. She had a voluptuous figure and was a glamorous woman. Glenda was her name Gentleman were her forte, even though she was happily married with three children to her husband, who was homosexual. Her husband agreed for her to have other men friends.

I was always a good listener. Late one night I received a telephone call from her daughter telling me Brenda had taken an overdose of tablets. I rushed down to see her and we called the ambulance. Everything turned out alright in the end. She continued with her two waitressing jobs and introduced me to dear Hugh, who was related to Gilbert - of Gilbert and Sullivan. I never paid much attention to this sort of music, especially Opera.

Hugh and I would go on the bus to British Home Stores for lunch and he would treat me to plaice, chips and garden peas once a week. I looked forward to it. I was also treated to an eighteen Carat gold sapphire and diamond ring as a Christmas present. Yes, old Hugh was generous to me until his daughter wanted him to sell the house and move to where she was living, which was understandable.

I was going to miss him when he left: old Hugh was like a father to me.

* * *

I tried to get home to Ireland once a year for a week's holiday to see my parents, but mostly my father. Every year I brought my daughter with me. Victor came when Jackie was nine, but only once. It was not for him. He was not always happy leaving his home.

The journey was long, travelling by train from Euston to Heysham, and then crossing the Irish Sea to Belfast. It was the same route I had to take from Ireland to England when I first came over.

On one of our trips I had left my stylish black coat behind on the train and we were just getting on the ship. I had to run back to the train, leaving my daughter with a train official. She was desperate with floods of tears when I returned. The tears soon passed with the excitement of the journey.

On checking in, we would go straight to our First

Class cabin. By this time it was after twelve midnight. Neither of us were ever sea sick and the Irish Sea can be rough. Travelling First Class was the only way to secure a cabin for the night.

As the ship approached the dock in the early morning we could see the mountains of Mourne sweeping down to the sea.

We could also smell the pungent stench of alcohol and sick on deck from all the passengers who stayed up drinking all night because they were not travelling First Class and had nothing else to occupy their minds apart from talking and boozing.

On arrival at the docks the crowds would clamber down the gang plank with their rough suitcases. Eddie was there to meet us. We would talk for a few hours and he would take us to the train station, where we would take the train from Omagh and then the bus to a place called Myra Cross where my sister, Etha would meet us.

Chapter 18

In April 1966 I went on my usual one week break over to Ireland by myself. In that week my father had a massive heart attack and died. His weight had escalated over the years and he was twenty-two stone when he passed.

It was an awful blow. The closest person I had, other than my daughter, had finally left me. He was seventy-seven.

No more would I see his cheerful face or smell his sweet tobacco. No longer would I watch him cleaning out his pipe with his little pen-knife sitting in the huge antique chair which I had bought him on my last visit.

With his spectacles on the end of his nose, he would look over and ask: *"How yer doin daughter? Are yer rightly now? Are you makin a wee drop of tae for me?"*

His light hearted words would never reach my ears again. There would be no more buying his tobacco when I came home; no throwing my arms around his neck so he would protect me from my mother. He was always on my side, even when I was in the wrong. He would spoil his pet - *"that naughty wee rascal"*.

He was Mr Thomas McCann, Big Tom - farm hand, road labourer, sometimes postman, and father of twelve children. He was now gone for good and was not returning.

The wake was held in the wee family house in Killymittan and the funeral service at Coa Chapel. The crowds of people that attended lined the country roads and the line of mourners seemed endless.

In a quiet moment I said to my sisters how terrible I felt about his death and that I was still in shock. A curt reply came back: *"We have all lost a father."* As my mother was living in the house with my brother Benny and his wife, to me there would no longer be a family home.

In the coming years ahead my husband and I rented a caravan in Fairlight, Sussex. My love of Ireland had gone with my father. The only memento my sisters and brothers had given me belonging to him was the little penknife that he used for cutting up his tobacco and cleaning out his pipe.

His death was such a profound loss that I would never quite recover from it. When mother died aged eighty-two in 1977, some years later, I did not suffer the same amount of pain.

I returned home to England soon after the funeral on an April Spring day. Turning on the radio, I heard the pop group Procol Harem singing '*A Whiter Shade of Pale'*. The following day I bought an E.P. record of it. Whenever I listened to this song I felt alone and an almost physical pain for the love of my father.

Not completely unexpectedly, I then had a nervous breakdown. My doctor, who was very understanding, prescribed me the controlled drug Dexedrine - an anti-depressant amphetamine tablet - together with sleeping tablets. This helped me relax and sleep, blotting out the sadness for a while.

I could not talk to my husband because he could be intolerant of bereavement and any other form of emotional distress. He just could not cope with them.

* * *

My daughter was now sixteen and too young to understand how I was feeling. Clothes and make-up were taking over her life. The only answer to my loss was pills and work, work and pills. Soon I was to become addicted to both; to this day I still take them.

Of course, there was no money left by my father, but I found out later that he had paid into an insurance policy, with mother receiving a small sum.

My brother Mickey witnessed the signature on the certificate after his death, and the age of death was inaccurate. It stated sixty, but he died aged seventy-seven. I smelt a fraud hanging in the air at that time.

My family in Ireland were dedicated churchgoers, attending Sunday Mass without fail, and always supporting funerals. Because of the constant church going routine, I found it hard to believe that they could not have found it in their hearts to give their father, whom they loved and respected, the courtesy of a headstone on his grave.

The graveyard was situated at the side and above the local Coa Church. The congregation would crowd into the little Chapel on Sunday and every week the family would pass the graveside. It took eighteen years for a headstone to be erected as none of my siblings had the decency to contribute to the cost.

Finally, when my second eldest brother John passed away with liver cancer, only then did his thoughtful wife and I set out to collect the money from each and every one of my brothers and sisters.

Later I went home twice to visit Ireland, only to find not one flower put on father's grave. What cold morsels and hypocrites families can be!

* * *

I had just one last visit to Ireland to see my relatives when both parents had long gone.

We were staying with my sister Etha, who suggested we take a trip to Mullaghmore, where Lord and Lady Mountbatten lived.

When we arrived we took a drive on a narrow road onto the beach and had to reverse on the beach when I had visions of sinking into the sand!

The Mountbattens owned an outstanding Neo-Gothic mansion in Sligo, in the north of Ireland, that had originally been built on the order of Lord Palmerston. Lady Mountbatten acquired the land in 1941, with she and Lord Mountbatten spending their holidays there in August. He was tremendously well liked by the locals and they welcomed them both with open arms. Thoughtfully, they allowed a local man to graze his cattle peacefully on their land.

In August 1979 the Mountbattens' and some relatives set sail on their twenty-nine foot boat named *Shadow V.* It was not long after it departed the little harbour of Mullaghmore when tragedy struck. A bomb blew up the boat; Lord Mountbatten died instantly.

My sister Etha knew some people who were sailing their boat at the time and they heard the sound of the bomb exploding. They came as quickly as they could to help, but by this time Lord Mountbatten was floating in the water, parts of his body dismembered.

The locals were left in pure numbness. When investigations got under way, no one admitted to seeing any person near his boat or around the area acting suspiciously.

* * *

No matter how short of money we were, we always ensured that we had a holiday every year for one week. We could not afford much so would usually hire a small shack of a caravan. We did not mind, we enjoyed every minute of it.

One caravan comes to mind. It was called *Dumbo* - small, grotty, but situated in countryside surroundings high on a clifftop with views overlooking a lake and the channel.

Enjoying the fresh air and away from the busy world of London, we would go walking along the cliff top at Fairlight Glen.

Some years later, after lodging endless students, we bought a second-hand larger caravan that Victor renovated slightly, which we used most weekends. We could be accompanied by our mongrel dog Pretzels and sometimes my nephew, James, would come too - just the four of us.

Chapter 19

My daughter was at Barnet College now and enjoying the change from school. She had a boyfriend who was studying Art and Design, so her time was taken up with studying, romance and going out.

It was time for me to have another job change now that we were living in north London. This next position was ideal for me, as it was just down the bottom of my road - a ten minute walk from our house.

Mr Jimmy Simmonds and his wife required a housekeeper and offered me the job. They were the older generation and had no children as they had decided not to adopt, so the house would be easy to keep clean. It was an attractive detached house with a pretty back garden with an ornamental pond, well maintained by the gardener whose nickname was Tuppence.

Mr Simmonds was a solicitor by profession and was educated at boarding school. He also had business interests in the Bahamas with his brother. Mrs Simmonds told me that she visited the Bahamas with her husband only once and vowed she had no wish to return. When they both booked a holiday it was normal for her to take her best friend along for company so that Mr Simmonds could play golf and she could spend her time doing other things. When she passed away Mr Simmonds asked me if I would stay on. It was an easy job as the house was immaculate and always tidy, so I did.

When he entertained his guests he would ask me to take on the cooking and lay the table. So one evening he wanted me to cook sole meunière. I had heard of it but had not a clue how to cook the fish dish. Standing over me at the cooker, he gave strict instructions what to do. This made me nervous. I laid the table with his Waterford glasses, white wine and silver. After the dinner was served, the guests complimented the chef.

Another day he asked me to prepare lunch for his brother, Sir Oliver Simmonds, and his wife, Lady Simmonds. I remarked to him that "there is only one Lady that I would respect and kneel down to and that is Our Lady in the Catholic Church."

He took heed of my comment as I heard no response.

Often he would chat to me and gave insights into his work. At one stage he had thirteen partners in a large firm of solicitors but now he was a consultant for a firm in Westminster. His political views were that of a staunch conservative and his idea was that the conservatives are there to *preserve*. He knew and respected Margaret Thatcher and felt she was the 'straightest' Prime Minister Britain had in a long time. His only reservation was that he felt she was selling off the family silver. He had firm views on politics, religion and Royalty.

Being in his position, he came into contact with various people and was partly responsible for smuggling the wife of Donald MacLean, the Russian Spy, into Russia by train. This he did by hiding her in the toilet.

"Where there is a will, there is a way" he used to say.

Apparently Guy Burgess and Donald MacLean both attended The RAC Club in Pall Mall, and had lunch together before defecting to the Soviet Union in 1951. I suppose it was to say goodbye.

Mr Simmonds had many heads. He had been the Governor of the Royal Marsden Hospital in Old Brompton Road, where he was well respected by the medical staff. He was concerned about the amount of money that was unaccountable on the NHS and tried to reorganise the expenditure.

In the 1960s Her Majesty the Queen came to the hospital to open a wing. I still have a black and white photograph of them both on the wall, given to me by Sir Oliver Simmonds.

One particular morning The Royal Marsden Hospital invited him to a visit so they could show him what changes had been made. He drove me in his pale blue Mercedes to the hospital, where we were greeted by all the doctors and nurses that lined the corridor on his behalf.

As he was out and about, he often did work in the

morning so I would visit for the afternoon. After the chores he would sit me down and offer a glass of sherry. He never forgot the sherry.

One afternoon he conveyed to me that he had lunch with the judge presiding over the Jeremy Thorpe (Liberal MP's) case. This case made much publicity in the Law Courts and newspapers at the time. Anyhow, the judge apparently told him that Mr Thorpe was going to 'get off', even though he remained guilty.

* * *

With the arrival of Summer, Mr Simmonds needed more of my help. He had been diagnosed with colon cancer for some years and wore a colostomy bag. He managed it very well with travelling to the Bahamas on his holidays. But his health was deteriorating and I helped to change the colostomy bag, which he was finding difficult.

I then went in during the morning making up his breakfast tray with a white linen cloth, a starched serviette, and Indian Tree bone china - just as he liked it. Toast, butter, marmalade and a pot of tea were neatly placed on top. We would then do the ablutions.

He died in 1981. At the funeral, Sir Oliver asked me to arrange refreshments. I also supplied the extra china, as there was not sufficient to go round.

As I was pouring the tea I overheard Mrs

Simmonds' best friend saying "If Jimmy had lived any longer, goodness knows what he might have left Mary Swannell". I assumed he had made a Will.

His loyal secretary of thirty-five years had been paid a very low wage for her services - something like thirty-five pounds per week. He was nowhere near generous to her financially, but because she was so loyal over the years (especially when he asked her to stay behind after a day in the office to cook and wait on the dining room table serving his business clients) she was left a substantial sum of one hundred and thirty five thousand pounds.

I remember making a comment to him one day and intimated that I would not mind having a holiday in the Bahamas. I was only joking, but he replied: "You will go Mary, someday."

I was surprised when I received a letter from one of his colleagues, a solicitor acting on his behalf, informing me he had bequeathed a legacy of *„Five thousand pounds in gratitude for the close care she has taken of me at home since I have been living alone.'*

I appreciated the gesture so much, but I never did take that trip to the Bahamas.

Chapter 20

I always seemed to be cleaning someone's house or looking after them, something I continued to do through to my seventies.

After taking care of Mr and Mrs Simmonds, I then crossed over the road to a lady friend of theirs, Mrs Sally Butcher. She had a good sized semi-detached house overlooking Friary Park Tennis Club and the Golf course. She had turned the house into two converted flats, with a gentleman tenant downstairs paying her rent whilst she lived upstairs with her black rescue cat, a thin little thing with quite a shabby coat.

Sally had two bedrooms, a lounge and a large kitchen. The lounge carpet was a striking Royal Blue that was covered from wall-to-wall with a thick layer of plastic. This was to prevent Kitty Kat from clawing at the pile. There was a litter tray in the kitchen, but the cat was getting on in years – sometimes it would have a little accident in the lounge.

The lounge was adorned with some interesting antique furniture, in particular an exquisite Dresden oval shaped mirror. This wonderful mirror was framed with little delicately placed flowers and I admired it every time. The instructions for cleaning this work of art were specific: I had to clean it with a soft paintbrush. In fact, cleaning just that one mirror took longer than it did to clean the rest of the flat.

Sally was married to Ernest Butcher and both had careers in the music halls in the 1950s when this type of entertainment was all the rage (Ernest had already passed away to the other side before I started working for his wife). She had been a singer and her voice carried on through the flat, serenading me whilst I was dusting. Pictures and photographs overpowered the room with her attractive costumes and pretty face, together with some famous theatrical people from the Music Halls

I could not help admiring her pendant chandelier, which she later gave me and still hangs in my hall. She was chatty and friendly. Often she would invite me to the Golf Club for a social drink in the afternoon.

Then one day pussy was feeling unwell and she asked if my daughter would kindly take the ailing cat to the veterinary clinic. On examination the vet felt it was really too old to make any recovery, and that it would be kinder for her to be put to sleep. My daughter returned with pussy and explained. Heartbroken Sally agreed to let the cat go back with my daughter and her beloved companion was put out of its suffering.

Sally had a fascinating life. Her father was Arthur Brough, a businessman who came to London in 1903 to take up an appointment with the Jaeger Wool Company. He had a day job in textiles, but also had evening engagements as a ventriloquist. Later his career exploded and he became a professional performer, appearing in Music Halls all over Britain. He had top billing as "Arthur Brough and Tim" - Tim being his ventriloquist dummy.

Sally had three sisters and two brothers. She met her husband during a Sunday evening at home when they were allowed to sit up a little later whilst their father entertained his friends. Within the group was Ernest Butcher, who later created the part of Mr Robinson on the radio called Front Line Family. When they finally married, Ernest performed in front of King Albert (Bertie), Queen Elizabeth and Princess Margaret.

One of her brothers, the famous Peter Brough Junior and his dummy (Archie Andrews), had a famous radio programme called *Educating Archie* that everyone loved. Lots of well-known stars (as we called them then) enhanced his life: Eric Sykes, Hattie Jacques, Max Bygraves, Julie Andrews, Beryl Reed and Harry Secombe - to name a few. The Golders Green Hippodrome staged Vere Lynn and Peter Brough. The list is endless. He married twice and had two children by his first marriage, then two other children from the second. I believe his second wife had been a model. Sally told me at one time they purchased a house in Virginia Water, which possibly belonged to Diana Dors the pin-up and actress.

Sally would reminisce about the good old days and was very proud of her brother. Seemingly always short of money, he would telephone her and she would always give in. Though he had a retail business in Saville Row selling gentleman's shirts, it could not have been that lucrative.

When I moved with my family to Bournemouth in the early 1980s Peter Brough wrote to me a few times - the first letter thanking me for all my help with his sister. The second time was to inform me that Sally had been admitted into a Nursing Home in Totteridge Lane. I never did hear from him again and assumed she died there.

* * *

Having a spare room gave me the idea to host foreign students for the summer. I was frugal and at times had two at a time.

We used the money to purchase a larger caravan, which my husband completely renovated. We took it regularly to the beautiful spot that overlooked a lake, cliffs and channel - a place we never tired of since Jackie was a baby.

Saturday morning Victor would to go the small shop on site and buy bread rolls, along with the Daily Mirror newspaper. Table freshly laid, a fry up was on its way: bacon, eggs, fried bread, sausages and tomatoes.

We would go down on Bank Holiday weekends and return late Sunday evening when the London traffic had subsided. The fresh air gave us an appetite. After breakfast we would go for a long walk, then on to Hastings Old Town for some local fish.

Package tour holidays were becoming popular amongst the working classes, giving us an opportunity to go abroad at little cost. Around January, when the winter was at its worst, Victor and I would spend two weeks going to Majorca from Gatwick Airport. My mother-in-law would dog-sit with Jackie.

Gradually we spent less time at the caravan and more time going to Spain. Victor was not happy with this arrangement, but we were growing apart.

Jackie was busy with her boyfriend, Clive, and going on their own holidays together.

I was devastated when she told me that she wanted to take up the job in Geneva to practice her French and to look after three children. Shock waves ran though Clive: marriage was out of the question now. They had been together since she was seventeen.

In November 1971 I was still working at The Orange Tree. One evening I had too much to drink; I was not usually a drinker but was upset. I did not want Jackie to leave me. I made a fool of myself and when I returned home burst into tears. I threatened to take an overdose if she left. *But she left anyway.*

I never telephoned her in Geneva as she was enjoying her freedom and I felt shut out. Her father mourned for a few weeks and slept in her bed.

Jackie returned in November 1972 when she received a telephone call in the morning. It was Clive's mother. Clive had been driving his MG Midget sports car and drove into the back of a lorry. The impact of the crash killed him instantly. Victor drove her to the scene of the accident. She felt embarrassed because Clive's wife was there as well.

The next sad death was that of Edwin Rapon, my previous employer, who died died aged fifty-six at the Whittington Hospital, north London. His funeral was held in Berkshire at his birthplace.

Chapter 21

In 1975, a few years after my daughter returned from Geneva, she re-started a job and saved her money. This enabled her to buy her own two-bedroom 1930s flat in North London, which her father stood as a guarantor for the mortgage.

The property needed a lot of 'doing up', as it had been let out previously. There was also money left over to put down a deposit on a small, brown Hillman Imp car, which she would also have to finance on hire purchase. So she had a lodger and students, which paid her father's wages to keep him employed.

She was stunned when her father went to visit her and announced that the marriage was not working and that he wanted to move to Fairlight, in Hastings, and buy a bungalow. He was aged fifty-six. It was not unexpected, although I cried and cried.

Jackie now had two of us to contend with and said she would sell her flat to help me out. I was not happy about her losing her independence though.

However, after moving to Sussex, Victor assured her that he would return and carry on with the painting and decorating if she needed the house painted, and do the odd jobs for me. He did not want a divorce. So he made an effort to temporarily move to Battle, then secured employment with an employer so he could get a mortgage. He and his dog (a Sheltie named Sandy - Pretzels had died by then) shared a bungalow overlooking the sea.

Meanwhile, I had to sell my lovely house. My daughter and I looked around the Finchley region but, on the wages I earned, I could not get a mortgage.

Jackie stepped in, put her flat up for sale and sold it to a young couple. She also arranged to buy her father's side of the house, which meant I could keep my home. The mortgage was set. Her flat was sold, but Victor had been gazumped on his seaside bungalow and, as usual, had no further funds to offer more on the sale price. Therefore I took him back: he was still my husband.

My daughter continued working and added to the profit she had made on the sale of her flat. In 1983 she bought her father a Vauxhall Chevette saloon car and a mink coat for me. After a lengthy discussion, we decided on a move to Bournemouth - *not* Hastings.

Mr Simmonds (before he died) gave me some invaluable advice: should the problem with Victor rear its ugly head again, I was to ensure my name was put on the Deeds of the property. When I married this was unheard of for women to worry about such detail.

We searched hard for somewhere in Bournemouth, then saw a large, three bedroomed detached house with lattice windows. We named it Magnolia Cottage because it had a Magnolia tree in the front garden. At the back there were lots of shrubs, apple trees and berry bushes. We paid

£46,000 in total and the house needed much refurbishment.

I took heed of what Mr Simmonds had told me and made an appointment with a solicitor to have my name on the Deeds of the property so I could leave half my share of the house to my daughter and all my worldly goods.

My husband had his own way in the end but the marriage had not been the same for a long time, so I did not expect the situation to change. We both had our home, which we wanted, and my Catholic faith helped me through prayer and made me strong. Victor concentrated on the decorating and gardening and I worked for a retired Jewish couple in an up-market area of Bournemouth. They needed a cleaner. Unfortunately the woman was incredibly fussy and only paid me one pound and sixty-five pence per hour. Even the bus fare cost more, and I was shattered by the time I came home.

When I announced one day that I wouldn't be returning to work for them, the husband drove me home in his dark green Rolls Royce.

One Sunday Mass a couple advertised in the newsletter for a person to do some cooking two hours a day, seven days a week. Mr Tom Andrews and his wife were incapable of doing this and Mr Andrews was partially blind. When his wife passed away he asked me to stay on. I would cook his lunch with a lid tied to the tea pot handle so he could feel it. For this work I was paid £50 per week.

Even as I got old myself, I was accustomed to always working and did not know what it was not to!

Victor did not work and retired at fifty-eight with very little money. He had to go on benefits as we still had bills to pay. From 1983 he gave me £30 per week and always paid for the turkey at Christmas. His remaining money went on cigarettes, dog food, and petrol for the car. My daughter paid his car insurance, tax, house insurance and took the brunt of running costs until he passed away. He had been happy in his own way and content with his lot.

Epilogue

This little story has come to an end now. When I started putting my thoughts down on paper, all my memories came flooding back; the good times and the bad.

I forgive all the people that I felt have been unkind, uncaring and did me wrong. And thank you to God for listening to my prayers when I prayed hard and long for my health to enable me to *keep going.* So I am proud that I have managed to put this book together of my eighty-six years, which has let me relive life through memories.

After my husband died of prostate cancer in July 2004 after much suffering, I often think about him. Maybe I should have tried harder in our marriage. Other times I feel 'guilty' that I did not treat him with more love, affection and respect.

I know now that I have only five weeks to live but can look back with a smile and know that it is time that I found peace and time to take a rest.

Tribute

By Mary's daughter Jackie

Mother passed away on 27th September 2006 after a short battle with cancer and died at home, where she wanted to be, with me taking care of her until the final end.

I am glad she wrote this little story, as a release. At times troubled, sometimes moody, occasionally aggressive and discontented, my mother was also a kind woman with a good sense of humour, generous, with a personality to match, who always took care of her appearance. She had well-creamed hands with immaculately varnished nails, smoked fifty Rothman cigarettes a day - not forgetting her cigarette holder.

She was a kind and thoughtful when people needed her most in their life. This is not to say that she did not find happiness in her own life – she did. But it was spasmodic. The passing of her father took her bright light away and a cloud seemed to follow her through life.

Her love for me was unconditional - so much so that nothing was too much for her to give me. Even when she was scrubbing other people's dirty floors to make some money, she would send me down to Bond Street in London to buy those Swiss Bally, Elliot or Kurt Keiger shoes. She always tried to give me the best that her purse could afford. When I was in College and had a problem; when I had a row with my boyfriend; when I took everything to heart. She'd say to me that life is not a bed of roses.

Even now I can hear her reciting that song:

"I beg your pardon, I didn't promise you a rose garden;
Along with the sunshine, there needs to be a little rain sometimes
So smile and let the world be jolly, life shouldn't be so melancholy
Think about all the good times that we shared..."

About the Author

Mary McCann was born in Northern Ireland in the 1920s - the third child in a large, poor, rural Irish family. Her journey was hard, often disappointing and above all challenging.

As a young woman she moved to North London, married and later moved to Bournemouth. She died in 2006. This is her story.

#0011 - 230718 - C0 - 203/127/9 - PB - 9781912092567